THE LIBRARY OF HOLOCAUST TESTIMONIES

Like Leaves in the Wind

D1614897

The Library of Holocaust Testimonies

Editors: Antony Polonsky, Sir Martin Gilbert CBE,
Aubrey Newman, Raphael F. Scharf, Ben Helfgott MBE

Under the auspices of the Yad Vashem Committee of the Board of
Deputies of British Jews and the Centre for Holocaust Studies,
University of Leicester

My Lost World by Sara Rosen
From Dachau to Dunkirk by Fred Pelican
Breathe Deeply, My Son by Henry Wermuth
My Private War by Jacob Gerstenfeld-Maltiel
A Cat Called Adolf by Trude Levi
An End to Childhood by Miriam Akavia
A Child Alone by Martha Blend
The Children Accuse by Maria Hochberg-Marianska and Noe Gruss
I Light a Candle by Gena Turgel
My Heart in a Suitcase by Anne L. Fox
Memoirs from Occupied Warsaw, 1942–1945
by Helena Szereszewska
Have You Seen My Little Sister?
by Janina Fischler-Martinho
Surviving the Nazis, Exile and Siberia by Edith Sekules
Out of the Ghetto by Jack Klajman with Ed Klajman
From Thessaloniki to Auschwitz and Back 1926–1996
by Erika Myriam Kounio Amariglio,
translated by Theresa Sundt
I Was No. 20832 at Auschwitz by Eva Tichauer,
translated by Colette Lévy and Nicki Rensten
My Child is Back! by Ursula Pawel
Wartime Experiences in Lithuania by Rivka Lozansky Bogomolnaya,
translated by Miriam Beckerman
Who Are You, Mr Grymek? by Natan Gross,
translated by William Brand
A Life Sentence of Memories by Issy Hahn,
foreword by Theo Richmond
An Englishman in Auschwitz by Leon Greenman
For Love of Life by Leah Iglinsky-Goodman
No Place to Run: The Story of David Gilbert by Tim Shortridge and
Michael D. Frounfelter
A Little House on Mount Carmel by Alexandre Blumstein
From Germany to England Via the Kindertransports by Peter Prager
By a Twist of History: The Three Lives of a Polish Jew by Mietek Sieradzki
The Jews of Poznań by Zbigniew Pakula
Lessons in Fear by Henryk Vogler
To Forgive . . . But Not Forget by Maja Abramowitch

Like Leaves in the Wind

RITA BLATTBERG BLUMSTEIN

VALLENTINE MITCHELL
LONDON • PORTLAND, OR

First Published in 2003 in Great Britain by
VALLENTINE MITCHELL
Crown House, 47 Chase Side
Southgate, London N14 5BP

and in the United States of America by
VALLENTINE MITCHELL
c/o ISBS, 5824 N.E. Hassalo Street
Portland, Oregon, 97213-3644

Website: www.vmbooks.com

Copyright © 2003 Rita Blattberg Blumstein

British Library Cataloguing in Publication Data
Blumstein, Rita Blattberg
    Like leaves in the wind. – (The library of Holocaust testimonies)
    1. Blumstein, Rita Blattberg – Childhood and Youth. 2. Jewish
    children in the Holocaust – Poland – Krakow – Biography
    3. World War, 1939–1945 – Deportations from Poland
    I . Title
    940.5'318'092

ISBN 0-85303-464-8
ISSN 1363-3759

Library of Congress Cataloging-in-Publication Data

A catalog record for this book is available from the Library of
Congress

Typeset in 11/13pt Palatino by FiSH Books, London WC1
Printed in Great Britain by MPG Books Ltd, Victoria Square,
Bodmin, Cornwall.

Dedicated to the memory of my
parents and grandparents.

Heureux qui, comme Ulysse, a fait un beau voyage…
Et puis est retourné, plein d'usage et raison,
Vivre entre ses parents le reste de son âge!

Joachim du Bellay

Contents

Illustrations

Between pages 74 and 75

Group I Before the War
1. Great-grandfather Aaron Schwarz.
2. Grandmother Estera (Erna) Schwarz Schreiber as a young woman.
3. Grandfather Abraham Schreiber with my Aunt Herminka Schreiber Diamand and my cousin Marcel. Kraków 1932.
4. Grandmother Leah (Laura) Landau Blattberg shortly before her death.
5. My Uncle Wolf (Wilek) Blattberg.
6. My mother Anna Schreiber Blattberg as a young woman.
7. Grandmother Schreiber with my cousin Romek. Kraków 1935.
8. Mother and friends in Zakopane.
9. My parents in late summer 1936.
10. Family vacation in Rabka.
11. Aunt Janka with my cousin Romek (Romeczek). Kraków.
12. Before the storm: with my friend Henryś Maj, a few weeks before the German invasion.

Group II The War
13. Myself, Lwów 1940.
14. Papa, Kambarka (1945?).
15. Telegram announcing survival of Grandmother Schreiber, Uncle Menek and Aunt Hela in Poland.

Group III Post-war
16. Myself in Kraków.
17. The three Schiff brothers in our apartment on Aleja Słowackiego.
18. The postwar Passover *seder* in our apartment on Aleja Słowackiego.
19. My cousin Marcel Diamand.

ix

The Library of Holocaust Testimonies

It is greatly to the credit of Frank Cass that this series of survivors' testimonies is being published in Britain. The need for such a series has long been apparent here, where many survivors made their homes.

Since the end of the war in 1945 the terrible events of the Nazi destruction of European Jewry have cast a pall over our time. Six million Jews were murdered within a short period; the few survivors have had to carry in their memories whatever remains of the knowledge of Jewish life in more than a dozen countries, in several thousand towns, in tens of thousands of villages and in innumerable families. The precious gift of recollection has been the sole memorial for millions of people whose lives were suddenly and brutally cut off.

For many years, individual survivors have published their testimonies. But many more have been reluctant to do so, often because they could not believe that they would find a publisher for their efforts.

In my own work over the past two decades, I have been approached by many survivors who had set down their memories in writing, but who did not know how to have them published. I realized what a considerable emotional strain the writing down of such hellish memories had been. I also realized, as I read many dozens of such accounts, how important each account was, in its own way, in recounting aspects of the story that had not been told before, and adding to our understanding of the wide range of human suffering, struggle and aspiration.

With so many people and so many places involved, including many hundreds of camps, it was inevitable that the historians and students of the Holocaust should find it difficult at times to grasp the scale and range of the events.

The publication of memoirs is therefore an indispensable part of the extension of knowledge, and of public awareness of the crimes that had been committed against a whole people.

Sir Martin Gilbert
(Merton College, Oxford)

Foreword

Like Leaves in the Wind needs no advertisement. It is a classic narrative of impossible times. Rita Blattberg Blumstein begins (and ends) her perfectly judged and impeccably written account with '30 yellowing postcards tucked inside a small paper box'. It is with such fragile and treasured artefacts that many of us measure out our lives, but there will be few among us who have had a life like the one described here. The postcards, written from Poland in 1940–41 and sent to the author and her parents at a forced labour camp in Soviet Russia, are only superficially about food parcels:

> Almost every card from Mielec and from Lwów is about packages; how to send them, what to send, what has arrived, what has been lost, what has been returned. It makes for tedious reading, but these postcards are not about literature. They are about love. It is a poignant irony that those who were about to die, the Blattbergs of Mielec and the Schiffs of Tarnów, gave their children a parting gift of life.

So the postcards are about more even than life and death. Unlike sex, love is not easy to write about. In this book it is written about so well that we are enabled to recover an understanding of its power for good, which in an increasingly loveless world we are on the verge of forgetting.

There is much else in the book that will give the reader pause. How striking, for instance, is the difference between German and Russian tyranny. The Soviet authorities deported people who for reasons of class they considered best out of the way. In Poland these were chiefly Poles, because the Poles were the governing elite, but Jews, Ukrainians, and Belorussians were also deported if they were defined as non-proletarian. The Nazi authorities were driven by racial considerations. They did not deport people to work, they deported Jews to be killed, left Russians to die, and murdered Poles, Ukrainians, and Belorussians on the slightest provocation or with no excuse whatsoever. There was also a rage to German racism missing from the class ideology of the Russians. How else is one to account for the massacre in Mielec on the eve of Rosh Hashana (13 September) 1939, when German soldiers 'herded Jews whom they took from the street into the main synagogue and two neighbouring prayer houses. They drove 35 naked men from the communal bathhouse into the ritual slaughterhouse, where there were already women who had brought chickens to be killed for the holiday meal. Everyone was burned alive, except for those who tried to escape and were shot.'

There was also a fury about the Polish antisemitism encountered by the author in Kraków on her family's return to their hometown in 1946. Postwar killing is well documented, although I do not know whether that which occurred at Tymbark south of Kraków, where the author's grandparents Schreiber came from and where during the war 'the Poles had butchered every single Jew in town – and then claimed the Germans did it – except for one boy who hid in the woods and lived to tell the story', is as widely known as those that took place in the Bialystok region in July 1941. 'And of course', the author says, 'I had my own experiences'. Here is one of them. At play with her Jewish classmates in the school yard, she was suddenly surrounded by older children who tripped her up and pushed her to the ground: 'the courtyard was covered with exceedingly sharp pebbles which made ugly gashes in both of my knees. I still have the scars from that day.' Her Jewish classmates were afraid to help; the two teachers on playground duty looked the other way. The girl who did come to her aid as she hobbled away was a Polish Girl Scout, who, when asked why she was helping 'this repulsive, mangy Jew-girl', replied that the Girl Scout code demanded that she 'look after plants and animals'. 'I had at last', says the author, 'found my rightful place in Polish society.' Is it any wonder that her family left for France early in 1948?

That story of common indecency reminds me of another. Hedi Fried recounts it in her book *Fragments of a Life*. A schoolgirl at Sighet in Transylvania, Hedi fell in love with a handsome boy she encountered on her way to and from school. In 1940 when she was sixteen and the Hungarians had annexed Transylvania from the Rumanians, one day for the first time she came across him on his own. 'My heart raced, my knees went weak. Now, now he will see me, perhaps he will greet me, perhaps even walk a few yards with me. He approached whistling, his eyes met mine and as we came level he spat...deliberately, with an expression of loathing, into my face.' It is a shocking passage. Was he Rumanian or Hungarian? It does not matter. A failure to greet another human being is the beginning of barbarism; to spit in another human being's face is barbarity itself.

Hedi Fried and Rita Blattberg Blumstein have been able to transcend their Holocaust experiences, but they have never got over the indignities inflicted on them in their early years. They were not small incidents. Historians believe that they can explain why Nazis killed Jews and Communists murdered peasants. They are no good at explaining why one child should deliberately hurt another, or why a boy should spit in a girl's face. The author's grandmothers, the writers of the postcards, which are published in the appendices to this invaluable book, would have been horrified at such unsocial behaviour. They were decent people. The author came across other decent human beings in Russia and in France, mostly uncouth country folk with the grace of spirit and generosity of mind that stems from living a life without ideology. I have no inclination to subscribe to the myth of rural innocence, yet it is evident that the perils of modernity are overwhelmingly urban in origin. Something, perhaps everything, went wrong in western Europe in the nineteenth century.

The terrifying events that occur off stage in this book are for the alert and sensitive reader all the more terrible because they happen in the wings. Rita Blattberg Blumstein has given us just one of the stories of the fall out from atrocity. She has told it with commendable coolness as well as clarity: her prose is always compelling, artless, direct, and never didactic. Her book must be read with careful attention, which, because that is how it has been written, is easily enough done.

Colin Richmond

Preface

While checking my father's documents in the days that followed his funeral, my husband and I found a stack of some 30 yellowing postcards tucked inside a small paper box. Made of coarse, porous paper, and blank on both sides, the cards are totally covered with tiny script which often overflows into the space reserved for the address and stamp.

These cards were written in 1940 and 1941, by my two grandmothers and a few other family members, and mailed to the Soviet forced-labor camp where my parents and I were detained at the time. We had been deported deep into the heart of Russia while most members of our family remained in occupied Poland, my grandmothers among them. Grandmother Blattberg was trapped by the Germans, in the western part of Poland that had been renamed Generalgouvernement, and Grandmother Schreiber was under the Soviets, in the eastern part that had been annexed to the USSR.

I was stunned by our discovery of the postcards. My parents had guarded them as a talisman throughout our endless displacements, yet no one had bothered to tell me of their existence, notwithstanding the many references to me, my grandmothers' beloved 'Ritusia', their *ptaszyna* – delicate little bird.

Why didn't my parents share these precious documents with me, their beloved and loving daughter? I was stunned and I felt cheated, but not surprised.

Like many families of Holocaust survivors we lived surrounded by a wall of silence. My father never spoke of anything from the past; he never even uttered his parents' names. Mother was somewhat more communicative, especially as she grew older, though even in her most unguarded moments she kept inner chambers of her memory tightly locked against intruders.

It is not for me to analyze the manner in which my parents dealt with their losses, but I must mention their silence in order to explain the gaps and omissions in this memoir. It is the story of the first ten years of my life and the story of my grandmothers' postcards mingled into one: a tiny fragment of the history of Polish Jews at the time of World War II.

The first and only child of Leon and Anna Blattberg, I was born in Kraków in 1937, two years before the beginning of the war. My coddled early childhood came to an end on the first day of September 1939 when the Germans invaded Poland and we were all sucked into the whirlwind of the destruction of Polish Jewry. We fled to the eastern, Soviet-occupied half of the country but were deported to Russia, as were over a million other Polish citizens – Jews and non-Jews – whom the Soviets considered politically unreliable. We were released from the forced-labor camp shortly after the Germans invaded the Soviet Union in June of 1941. After an epic journey to Astrakhan on the Caspian Sea, we unexpectedly reversed direction and ended up in a village in the west-central Urals, where we lived until our return to Kraków in April of 1946.

By March of 1948 we were living in Paris. I became very French, burying Poland into my subconscious. In 1960, now married and a graduate student, I sailed with my husband for a two-year stay in the United States; the director of our research institute in France was 'keeping our places warm' until our return. However, we soon fell into the gravitational pull of America and built our life there. Our two daughters were born in Massachusetts, yet, ironically, our younger daughter has been living in Paris for more than ten years.

My parents remained in France and they are both buried there, alone under the Mediterranean sun on a hilltop overlooking the magnificent Bay of Angels, the bay of Nice. To my knowledge, not a single member of my family remains alive in Poland, though there are records documenting the uninterrupted presence in Kraków of my paternal grandmother's ancestors for almost 500 years.

My mother and her first cousin, David [Duduś] Schiff, are my primary sources of information concerning my early childhood and the events of the war. My husband and I have recorded their testimonies on tape in order to complement the information that I had already gleaned from them and from other surviving relatives.

I came to know my grandparents through their postcards, which I spent a long time deciphering. They are written in Polish or in German, the latter in the ornate Gothic script. Although I know both languages, I could make little sense of the text at first: the characters are tiny, since my grandmothers were most anxious to cram as much information as possible into the small space allotted to them; the script is old-fashioned, punctuation is almost non-existent and names of persons are abbreviated. At last, patterns began to emerge in my grandmothers' individual way of writing this or that letter or syllable, and the text suddenly made sense – with the exception of two cards that must have been made wet by rain or tears and where the ink had bled.

My grandmothers' postcards, as well as other documents that my parents have preserved, are beyond price to me. They are also of value to historians who continue to be interested in the life of Polish citizens deported to the USSR following the 1939 annexation by the Soviets of the eastern half of Poland – and the contacts that existed between the deportees and those left behind in occupied Poland, under the Germans in the west and the Soviets in the east. This niche of history is rather hotly debated at present, in light of the release of NKVD archives after the collapse of the Soviet Union. Even the numbers of those deported seem to be uncertain, with recent estimates ranging from about 800,000 persons to two million families.

My parents kept their postcards with their most intimate papers for me to find after their death: this is 'the last card we have received from my parents,' Papa wrote on a card from Mielec dated May 28,1941. 'This is Leib Blattberg,' he wrote on a tiny passport-size picture of my grandfather that we found with the postcards. 'And this is Laura Blattberg,' he wrote on his mother's picture, speaking to me from beyond the grave. In life he could not bring himself even to say his parents' names.

This, then, 'is Leib Blattberg, and this is Laura Blattberg' as they speak to me through their postcards. May their souls rest in peace forever – and the souls of the Landaus, the Blattbergs, the Schwarzes and the Schreibers, the Schiffs and the Wassertheils who died during the war.

Acknowledgements

My husband Alex – my life's companion for almost 45 years – has encouraged me from the moment that I sat down to decipher the tiny hieroglyphics on my grandmothers' postcards. This memoir could not have been written without him by my side. He stood by me at every step of this writing, and gave me the strength to reconstruct my grandparents' painful fate and, through their story, to relive the destruction of the Jews of Mielec.

My daughters Sylvie and Tanya, and my son-in-law Uri have read the first draft of my manuscript. The revised version owes much to their loving and insightful suggestions.

I also wish to thank the dear friends who have read the manuscript and made helpful suggestions. I am grateful to Louise Hulks, my editor at Vallentine Mitchell, for her invaluable help. Last, but not least, I am grateful to Felicity Bloch of Melbourne, to Professor Irene Eber of the Hebrew University of Jerusalem and to Professor Shimon Redlich of Ben-Gurion University. They have sent me precious references and documents, including the memoir of Jozef Mądry and copies of the official German records on the March 9, 1942 *Aktion* against the Jews of Mielec.

Among the many colorful, pithy Yiddish curses, perhaps none is more colorful than the invective, 'May you live in interesting times.' Since I grew up during extremely 'interesting' times indeed, the reader might wish to learn more about the historical events which have shaped my childhood. Thus, I have included in the 'Notes and References' section, a very incomplete list of references concerning topics such as the Soviet conquest of eastern Poland and the subsequent deportations of Polish nationals or the situation of Jews in interwar Poland.

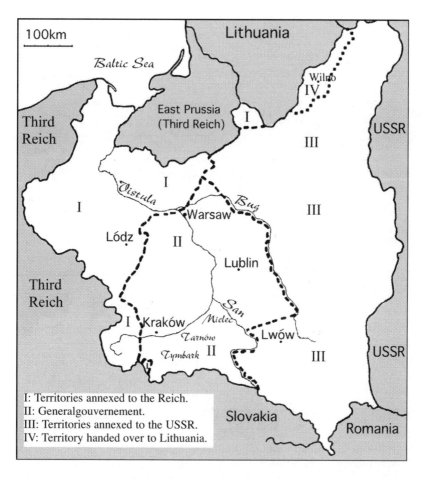

I: Territories annexed to the Reich.
II: Generalgouvernement.
III: Territories annexed to the USSR.
IV: Territory handed over to Lithuania.

Map 1. Partition of Poland, September 1939

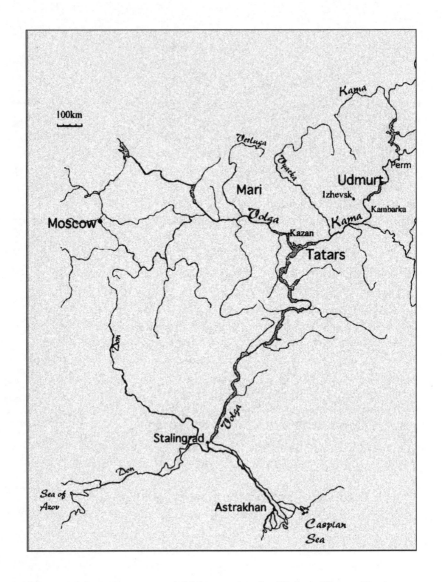

Map 2. Mari, Tatars and Udmurt in the Volga–Kama Basin

1   *Little Anna*

All I know about my maternal grandfather Abraham Schreiber is that he was born in 1880, somewhere in western Galicia, the southern part of Poland that was then a province of the Austro-Hungarian empire.

Abraham was still in his teens when he met Estera Erna Schwarz, the girl who was to become his wife and my grandmother. Estera had lost her mother at a very early age, but her father had remarried and produced several more children. This noisy crowd of siblings and half-siblings – Salo, Herman, Rachela, Estera, David, Sarah, Leib – lived west of Kraków in the small Galician town of Chrzanów.

One day, as he was traveling to Chrzanów on business, Abraham attended Friday night services at the synagogue where my great-grandfather Aaron Schwarz was worshipping. The custom of the time dictated that hospitality be extended to lonely travelers and so it happened that Grandfather Schreiber ate his *Shabos* Eve meal at the Schwarzes.

It was love at first sight by the light of Friday night candles. Buxom, blond and blue-eyed, with a high forehead and broad Slavic cheekbones, Estera was renowned for her beauty. The townspeople called her 'Piękna Esterka' [the beautiful Esterka]. As for Abraham, he was handsome in a more 'Jewish' way, his eyes dark and almond-shaped. He was slim and dignified, a quiet, soft-spoken man well-versed in the Talmud.

It was not an era of protracted engagements, so a proper Jewish wedding was soon celebrated. My Aunt Herminka was born before Estera's nineteenth birthday. Next came my Aunt Janka, my Uncle Menachem (Menek), and – on December 29, 1909 – my mother, Hannah (Anna), the youngest of the Schreiber siblings.

Mother was born in Tymbark, a very small town located in the Limanowa district south of Kraków, where Grandfather managed a sawmill and a timber forest that belonged to a wealthy Polish count. Grandfather was a hardworking, capable man, with a passion for his trees of pine, spruce and fir. His timber was of exceptional quality, suitable for niche markets such as the shipmasts which he exported to Prussian shipyards. He saved every penny and, at about the time of Mama's birth, he was able to purchase his very first parcel of forest. He planted there neat rows of saplings while at the same time continuing logging and planting in the forest that he leased from the count.

With the outbreak of World War I in August of 1914, the business came to a standstill. Huge piles of unsold timber rotted by the railway sidings, while fierce battles raged all around the Schreibers. In the ebb and flow of the Austro-Hungarian and tsarist armies, Grandfather lost everything that he had so painstakingly acquired.

Just as the war was ending at long last, after more than four years of carnage, the deadly pandemic of Spanish influenza swept the country. In the streets of Tymbark, at the sawmill and in the market square, men and women in their prime were keeling over as if felled by lightning – and, incredible as it might seem, they died more swiftly and in greater numbers than the old or the very young. Grandmother kept busy from dawn to dusk cooking huge pots of soup that she lugged to the bedside of sick peasants or shopkeepers, until the day when Grandfather collapsed as well and nearly died. He recovered – a diminished man with a permanently weakened heart.

Life eventually returned to something approaching normality, though for the Jewish minority it was fraught with danger now that Poland had regained its independence after nearly 150 years of partitions. Pogroms and widespread looting proclaimed the return of Polish rule: a period that the Jews nicknamed 'the time when Poland broke out' – in antisemitic violence. Yet Mama was a child, and the family was not directly affected in the beginning. Little Anna was growing up surrounded by the natural beauty of the countryside around Tymbark, in the scenic foothills of the Tatry mountains. She drank in the splendor of the mountains, rivers, valleys, and the forests filled with mushrooms and wild berries. She idolized her father, whom she followed to the forest whenever he would let her.

Shortly after the return of Polish independence, notwithstanding the economic boycott imposed on Jews in the new Poland, Grandfather was able to purchase a second parcel of land. He planted it with saplings from a nearby nursery. 'I stood there with Papa as he knelt down and gently patted the earth around his trees, as if they were his babies,' Mama told us in a tape-recording that we made two or three years before her death, when her body was already ruined but her mind still clear.

'*Nasz las by*ł *taki piękny* [Our forest was so beautiful.] It was full of wild strawberries', she continued, her voice filled with childish wonder. And she added: 'Papa said that I brought him luck because he was able to buy this land despite all the restrictions against Jews owning property in the new Poland. He registered the land in my name, or Janka's name, I can't remember which. He said that the trees would be for his grandchildren to harvest.'

Mama spent her childhood in Tymbark among the local Polish population. She attended the village school. There were only seventeen Jewish families in Tymbark and, like most Polish Jews, they barely managed to keep body and soul together. They ran miserable little shops, mere holes in the wall.

'*Nędzaże; taka bida z nędzą*' [They were so destitute, such misery and destitution], Mama used to say. The most 'prosperous' was a Mrs Bek, whom Mama called 'Bekowa' according to the Polish way, by adding the suffix -*owa* to the husband's name in order to signify 'the wife of'. Bekowa, who sold notions and fabric by the yard, would occasionally travel to Nowy Sącz or to Kraków to replenish her stock and was thus considered 'wealthy' because she was able to afford the train ticket for the 75-kilometer journey to Kraków. However, she had to borrow money from Grandfather for the few bolts of fabric that she needed to buy.

Bekowa did most of her business on Monday, the market day in Tymbark. Come Monday, as soon as she had sold enough fabric, she would run to the Schreiber house to repay

Grandfather, and the following week, or the week after, she would be back to borrow a bit more. It was a typical *shtetl* scene, although the little town of Tymbark was not considered a *shtetl* because nearly all the inhabitants were Polish.

Despite Grandfather's best efforts, crisis followed crisis. One day, as he and his forester were marking off trees for cutting, a lynx jumped down from a branch, breaking the forester's neck and instantly killing him. Then, in the early 1920s, after the Soviet Union was formed, the Russians began the practice of dumping timber on the Western market at prices that Grandfather could not even remotely match. The export market to Germany collapsed when the plague of hyperinflation came to the Weimar Republic. Mama used to play in the family attic with trunks full of the worthless German currency, of 'which one needed a full trunk just to buy a loaf of bread'.

And, as if that were not enough, rabidly antisemitic anonymous letters – which Mama called *czarna ręka* [the black hand] – began to circulate around Tymbark. Grandfather, who was relatively well-off, in contrast to the poverty-stricken Jews of this tiny community, was singled out and accused of all manner of evil deeds. The family feared for their lives, and with good reason, for the Poles were so primitive in their hatred of the Jews that even the most incredible tales were readily believed.

The business survived somehow. The count agreed to sell Grandfather the sawmill and a plot of land near the railway. Grandfather made a downpayment. All of the papers required to finalize the sale were ready at the local district court in Nowy Sącz. With the count's permission, Grandfather built a storage hangar for his timber, as well as a railway spur leading directly from the sawmill to the station. He designed and supervised everything himself, even the electrical wiring.

Meanwhile the count, who like many among the Polish gentry preferred leisure to hard work, was spending the winter on the French Riviera. He died there suddenly of a heart attack before affixing his final signature to the deed. His widow refused to honor her husband's commitment. Prodded by her two brothers, who were active members of the rabidly anti-Jewish Endecja Party,[1] she would allow Grandfather to continue running his business only for the term remaining in the original lease.

Grandfather went to court. He won his case twice, first in the district court in Nowy Sącz and then in Kraków. Unfortunately, the countess's son had Endecja connections at the appeals court in Warsaw, where Grandfather lost everything – the fruit of his lifetime labor. He suffered his first heart attack during this period.

The Schreibers were ruined, but – in an ironic twist of fate – the count's family suffered their own misfortune when their only daughter had an affair with the estate bookkeeper, who got her pregnant and infected her with raging syphilis that resisted treatment.

After losing their appeal in Warsaw to the countess and her Endecja connections, the Schreibers moved to an apartment on Jasna street in Kraków. Grandfather, a middle-aged man with a bad heart, now had to start all over again.

Even though Grandfather was an observant Jew, Mama went to a *Państwowe Gimnazjum*, a Polish state high school, rather than a Jewish school. Polish was spoken at home, but everyone was able to communicate in Yiddish because Yiddish was the language of the poor who formed the majority of the Jewish population.

Grandmother kept a kosher home. The traditional Sabbath meal on Friday night was the highlight of the week. Even after the three daughters were married they continued to come on Friday nights along with their husbands. Aunt Herminka married a lawyer, Lonek Diamand. Aunt Janka married a first cousin from Tarnów, Jules Wassertheil, the son of one of Grandmother's half-sisters. Mama's engagement followed in short order.

Only Uncle Menek remained a bachelor until the late 1930s. The only son, he was expected to acquire a profession, but he steadfastly refused to study. At some point, in sheer desperation, Grandfather even went so far as to tie him to the dining room table to force him to stay put with his school books. Nothing helped. Headstrong and rebellious, Menek never completed his studies, but he was quick-witted and resourceful and very knowledgeable about forestry. He felt perfectly at ease among the countryfolk, with his peasant ways and his straw-blond hair that Mama called ' blond as a pig', to contrast it with the lustrous gold of Grandmother's tresses.

Yet had Menek looked more Jewish, had he been more interested in his studies than in timber and sawmills, he would not have been able to survive under the Germans, nor carry his mother on his back when she could no longer walk. Though everything seems so obvious to those of us who look back with hindsight, who expected the Shoah in the Kraków of the 1920s? Who could have imagined that the Germans would cut down for the Wehrmacht the trees of Tymbark that Grandfather had planted for his grandchildren?

As the 1930s rolled in, Grandfather's health continued to deteriorate. He had to stay indoors for extended periods of time because his angina pectoris was so bad that he could not catch his breath in the cold winter air. In 1931 or 1932, my grandparents moved from Jasna street to an apartment on Agnieszka street, which was supposedly better for Grand-father's health. This apartment was located on the path of the funeral procession for Marshal Pilsudski[2] as he was brought to rest at the Wawel castle after his death in May of 1935. The funeral was grandiose. All those who lived on the path of the funeral procession were ordered to light candles in their windows in honor of the fallen hero. When a policeman came ringing my grandparents' doorbell to make sure that their windows were properly illuminated, Grandfather became frightened at the sight of the uniform – not an unreasonable reaction given the antisemitic violence which erupted in the wake of Pilsudski's death.

One can say that Grandfather died of fright, because he suffered a fatal heart attack at the sight of the policeman. He was 55 years old. Mama, who was watching the funeral procession from a relative's window on Basztowa street, did not have a chance to say goodbye to her beloved father. She mourned him for the rest of her life, even after her mind began to drift during her final years.

Antisemitism worsened considerably after Pilsudski's death. One day in 1938, my cousin Marcel Diamand came home from school beaten to a bloody pulp. 'Nobody is going to lift a finger against my Marcelek ever again,' screamed his father. He marched off to the Argentinian embassy, where he bought an immigration visa with an appropriately placed bribe, and he left for Buenos Aires with the intention of establishing a beachhead there before sending for his family. My Aunt Herminka, my cousin Marcel and his little sister Anita were about to leave for Buenos Aires, their visas and their steamship reservations in hand, when Marcel became very ill with scarlet fever. By the time he recovered, the Germans were already in Kraków.

Almost no one in my family had enough foresight to leave Poland before it was too late, except for a handful who went to Palestine out of Zionist conviction and a few who moved to France after World War I. My own parents went on a cruise to Scandinavia in the summer of 1939, when it was perfectly clear that war was imminent. They left me with my nanny and my grandmother, who was taking the waters in Krynica for her ailing stomach.

'It was bizarre,' Mama was fond of telling me. 'Entire families were on board, even with small children.' This was indeed peculiar, as it was the custom in those days to leave small children at home with their nannies.

'When we docked in Copenhagen,' Mama went on, 'these families went on shore but did not come back on board. That was when we understood what was happening.'

'Why didn't you stay too, instead of coming back to the war?' I would ask.

'Because we didn't want to leave you,' Mama would invariably reply.

This was one of my favorite stories, and I never tired of hearing it. It was so reassuring to hear, again and again, that my parents returned straight into the maw of the German beast in order to rescue me.

My parents came back shortly before the German invasion, bringing with them a completely naked doll which Mama called Falunia – the girl of the waves. Falunia went with me everywhere in our wanderings, dressed in a pale blue frock with white polka dots and a lovely lace collar that Mama later sewed for her – that is until I lost her on a raft somewhere on the Volga. Perhaps she was stolen.

Falunia was not purchased naked. She had actually been bought in Copenhagen wearing a lavish frock and underpants trimmed with lace. Mama, afraid of wrinkling the dress by crushing it in her luggage, removed it from the doll. While she was at it, she also removed the doll's frilly underpants. (Mama was the type of person who never left well alone.) She was about to slip the dress and the panties into the soft pouch that protected her silk scarves and her silk stockings when she noticed a large bowl of fruit standing on a small table. It was filled with apples, pears and oranges, each wrapped in fancy tissue paper. Mama unwrapped some of the fruit and wrapped the doll's dainty clothing in the tissue paper. She put everything on the bed and turned her back for a moment, just as Papa was entering the cabin to take a nap. When Mama turned around a few seconds later, Falunia's dress was gone, thrown overboard through the open porthole. Papa had seen all the tissue paper lying on the bed and proceeded to tidy up in manly fashion. (Lest anyone be tempted to think that Papa was a careless polluter of the ocean, let me say that he was not; it was simply that in those distant days ships disposed of their trash by throwing it overboard so that, fastidious as he was, Papa thought nothing of throwing a few bits of tissue paper into the sea.)

The loss of Falunia's wardrobe to the sea was a prelude to the disappearance of our own wardrobes, and all our possessions, a few weeks later. But let me first introduce the Landau and Blattberg side of the family.

2 'Rice-with-Milk'

My father, Leiser [Leon] Blattberg, was born on January 28, 1901 in the small town of Mielec, in Austrian Galicia. In contrast to Tymbark, which was overwhelmingly Polish, Mielec was a typical *shtetl*, that is a small town where Jews were numerous or even in the majority. Just as in any *shtetl*, most of them were poor, often destitute, and lived from hand to mouth with a bit of help from the Jewish community.

The Blattbergs, however, were privileged landowners. My great-grandparents owned a *dwór*, a country estate, in the nearby village of Gliny Wielkie, a name that means 'the Big Clays'. The 1928 land registry lists my Great-grandmother Chava Blattberg, who was already a widow by then, as the largest landowner there. The family also owned a large house located at Rynek 17 [17 Market Square] in Mielec.

Every Polish town has a *rynek*, the traditional heart of the community. The house at number 17 was among the biggest in town, 'so big,' Papa told us once, 'that it had its own *shtibl*' [small synagogue].

'On *Shabes* afternoons,' he added, 'the men would gather in the parlor while the girls of the house served refreshments.' This description, which speaks volumes about the status of women in *shtetl* society, also reminds me that Papa actually did talk to us once or twice as he began reminiscing shortly before his death, but only on peripheral issues, never uttering his parents' names, much less how they lived or died.

How pale is Papa's brief mention of *Shabes* afternoons at Rynek 17 when compared to the colorful description of the very same household in Mark Verstandig's memoir, *I Rest My Case!*[1] Young Mark studied the Talmud – both Mishnah and Gemorah – in a nearby yeshiva and, as was then the custom, on *Shabes* afternoons he visited the home of a learned notable in order to be quizzed on his knowledge. About his early adolescence in the Mielec of the 1920s, Mark Verstandig writes:

> Every Saturday afternoon during my two years at the Borower Rabbi's yeshiva I took turns to visit one of two local dignitaries, Reb Nissan Henekh Nussbaum and Idl Cohen, for an 'examination' of a page of *Gemore*, which I had learned the preceding week... Idl Cohen had married into the wealthy family of the Blattbergs,* who owned a large estate in the village of Gliny Wielkie... He was tall and well-built, his beard closely trimmed without sidelocks. Although he wore a black silk coat to the synagogue on *Shabes*, he preferred an elegant modern velvet hat to the traditional fur-edged *shtraymel*. He spoke good Yiddish and Polish. With an income from the [Blattberg] family estate, he was free to pursue his intellectual interests, and it was widely known that he read and studied voraciously. His three daughters had taken medical degrees, probably abroad, since Jews were rarely admitted into medical schools in Poland... They emigrated to Palestine and were among the founders of the Hadassah hospital [in Jerusalem].
>
> Initially, my *Shabes* examinations with Idl Cohen followed a set pattern. When the test was over he would offer me a biscuit, some nuts, or cooked peas. [These must have been the 'refreshments' that Papa alluded to – the 'cooked peas' were boiled chick-peas, a favorite *shtetl* delicacy.]
>
> One day, Idl Cohen suddenly asked me what I had been reading that week. Cautiously, I asked what he meant. 'I mean, simply, books, novels.' I reflected that, since he already knew, I might as well confess.

Young Mark was 'confessing' to the sin of reading secular literature, in this particular instance, a Yiddish translation of *Les Misérables*. But far from scolding the boy, Idl Cohen engaged him in a discussion of the forbidden story. 'He questioned me about the book, interrupting our discussion to

---

*He was married to Papa's aunt, Reisel Blattberg.

say the afternoon prayers. Then he kept me for *shalashides* (the third meal of the Sabbath day)...My subsequent visits every second week were more taken up by literature than by the quota of *Gemore* from the previous week.'

Although ten years older than Mark Verstandig, my father had a similar upbringing. Young Leon Leiser, my father, also went for his weekly *Shabes* afternoon 'examination' on a portion of the *Gemore*. He once told my older daughter and her fiancé that, no matter how well he performed on his 'examinations', he was never complimented for his efforts. Such was the way of the *shtetl*. Father applied the *shtetl* spirit to my own upbringing, inasmuch as he never complimented me for things well done – not once – for as long as he lived.

My grandfather Leib Blattberg was the oldest of twelve children – Leib, Mendel, Reisel, Chaia, Shulem, Gisela, Jakob, Hannah, Meilech, Sarah, Benjamin, and Rachel – the six sons and six daughters of Chava Hermele and Alter Blattberg. It is not clear how Chava managed to raise twelve children, but it seems that her brood often drove her to distraction because she was famous for her habit of grabbing hold of her head in desperation and exclaiming, '*Der Kop starczyt me nish!*' [This is all too much for my head!]

In contrast to the Verstandigs, who were a traditional Hassidic family where strict orthodoxy prevailed, Alter and Chava Blattberg seem to have tolerated a degree of secular learning. One of the Blattberg dozen, my Great-aunt Sarah, later wrote in her recollections:

My father, blessed be his memory, was an exception [to the then prevailing strict orthodoxy] by being in favor of secular education, too. He wanted us to be educated in Talmud and Torah, of course, but also in secular studies, so he hired the best teachers for the boys and private tutors for both the boys and the girls. These tutors taught us different subjects such as History, Geography, German and Polish and their literatures, and also modern Hebrew. I became very interested in Zionism and had an opportunity to attend a Zionist Congress in Vienna.

The only photograph we have of Grandfather Leib is a tiny photocopy from an identity card, where his occupation is listed as that of *kupiec* (merchant) and from which it is hard to judge how he really looked, except that he had dark eyes and hair. The 'Blattberg mouth', the blue eyes and fair complexion that have been passed on to my grandson Benjamin, belong to my Grandmother Laura.

Laura Blattberg, whose Hebrew name was Leah, was born to a branch of the Landau family that had lived in Kraków for almost 500 years. They had initially come from Altoona, near Hamburg, when Altoona was still part of the Danish kingdom and they were among the leaders of the Jewish community in Kraków. Thus my great-grandmother was one of two little girls chosen to present a bouquet of flowers and curtsy to the Austrian emperor Franz Josef upon his official visit to Kraków – one little girl representing the Polish and the other the Jewish community, a perfect metaphor for the parallel lives of the two peoples.

In the golden age for Jews of Galicia, during the reign of Emperor Franz Josef, the Landaus probably straddled the fence between traditional and secular learning. My Great-aunt Gisela Landau was among the first women awarded a doctorate at the Jagiellonian University of Kraków, but others seem to have clung to Talmudic scholarship, and the women by and large tended to stay 'in their place'.

Great-grandfather Landau was a widower who had an unmarried daughter keep house for him. He would get up every morning at dawn, rather noisily, and do what old men do before chanting his morning prayers. His sleep-deprived daughter once asked him, 'Papa, why do you get up so early every day?'

'*Bis du shon geveysen an alte Yid?*' [Have you ever been an old Jew already?] was his answer – a question for a question, in Talmudic style.

Two generations later, Papa used the same phrase to fend off the timid comments we sometimes ventured to make about his rigid lifestyle.

I don't know the exact number of Landau siblings, but I think there were four daughters and three sons. In addition to Gisela Landau and the unmarried daughter who kept house for Great-grandfather, Grandma Laura had a sister named Golda (Gusta) Gretzer, who lived in Kraków, and whom we shall later meet as one of our postcard writers. Through Gusta and Laura's postcards, we shall also become acquainted with my Great-uncle Szymek Landau and his wife, Binka. Another Landau brother and his wife had been killed in an accident long before the war. Their two young children, Tulek (Naftali) and Hela Landau were raised by Szymek and Binka, who had no children of their own.

Grandmother Laura was a reluctant Mielecer, and probably felt stifled in the oppressive *shtetl* atmosphere. She was an avid reader who would set her soups to simmer and her cakes to bake on their own while she sat at the kitchen table, engrossed in her books. '*Gotuj się, bakuj się*' [Cook by yourself, bake by yourself], she would exhort her pots and her pans.

The phrase '*Gotuj się, bakuj się*', is a mishmash of Polish, Yiddish and German. Among the more privileged, everyone was fluent in several languages, the Yiddish of the poor *shtetl* dwellers as well as Polish and German. Papa certainly could switch seamlessly from one to the other, and he also spoke and wrote Hebrew very well. His German was perfect and, having gone to school in Vienna during World War I, he spoke it with a pure Viennese accent.

Grandmother Laura and young Leon lived in Vienna as refugees from the war while Grandfather Leib was fighting in Austrian uniform, since the Jews of the Austro-Hungarian empire were drafted and fought in proportion to their numbers in the population. Papa's older brother, my Uncle Wolf (Wilek), was probably in Vienna as well. He eventually became a teacher at the Hebrew High School in Kraków in the interwar period, a position for which he was vastly overqualified, with his two PhD degrees. In this he was not alone, because Jews in the newly independent Poland were barred from most university positions, indeed from studying at a university – except for the few admitted under a strict *numerus clausus* (quota), and who were forcibly segregated into the back of the classroom, the 'bench ghetto', where they were often assaulted with clubs and switchblade knives.

Schooled in Vienna, Papa could not even apply to a Polish university, for lack of the *matura* degree, the certificate of graduation from a Polish high school. It was just as well: a timorous man, afraid of confrontation and verbal or physical violence, Papa was ill-suited to braving the Endecja thugs who terrorized Jewish students in interwar Poland. His parents could have afforded to send him to study abroad, but Papa preferred to work in his uncle's textile business. Yet, having started school at the age of three in a *heder* where boys were ruthlessly drilled in Hebrew and the Holy Books, he continued to learn on his own for the rest of his life. He had an excellent memory and a sharp, though conventional, mind. He read in five languages – Polish, Hebrew, Yiddish, German and French – and even taught himself some English when already an old man in his late eighties.

Just as paleontologists manage to reconstruct an entire dinosaur from the finding of a few bones, so must I try to recreate the atmosphere of my grandparents' house in Mielec from a few words and phrases. *'Ryzu z mlekiem'* (a child's way of saying 'Rice-with-milk'), my father's nickname in childhood, is one of these phrases and, because it is in Polish, I am assuming that Polish was the primary language in the Blattberg household, or at least the language used for basic events such as family meals.

Yet Yiddish must have been for Papa the language of the heart because he reverted to it in moments of distress and he often used it to cow us into psychological submission. Whenever I dared to ask a question he wouldn't answer, he would launch into his famous tirade: *'Erbarm doch, Erbarm doch! Wos wilst du frum mi'e huben?'* [Have pity on me, have pity on me! What do you want from me?], but usually only after the Polish equivalent of *'Daj mi spokój'* [Leave me in peace!] had failed to work.

At the same time, the sweetest sound of my childhood was his rarely uttered Yiddish word *'Kindleben'* [Child of my life]; more often than not, he called me his *'Hojkier'* [Literally a hunch, as in 'hunchback', a burden, a deformity that one is saddled with].

Papa must have made family dinners in Mielec rather difficult through his adamant refusal of most foods. He wouldn't so much as taste meat for years, demanding to be fed his beloved '*Ryzu z mlekiem*' day after day. He eventually learned to like meat as well, but he remained fussy and unadventurous, refusing 'anything that he hadn't tasted at his grandmother's house'. Given Grandma Laura's lack of enthusiasm for the culinary arts, it is hardly surprising that he ate most of his meals at his Grandmother Chava's table.

Great-grandmother Chava, who was a widow, lived in the family house at Rynek 17 in an apartment located above that of Leib and Laura. One day, an employee from the census bureau came to call on Chava with paperwork to fill out for the comprehensive 1931 census. Great-grandmother told the census-taker that she was 60-years-old.

'How can that be, Mrs Blattberg?' the man asked her in amazement. 'I was just downstairs in your son's apartment, and he is 59!'

'Oh, don't pay any attention to him,' replied Great-grandmother. 'He is a fool who does not know what he is saying.'

No, Great-grandmother Chava was not senile – she still had all her wits about her when the Germans killed her some ten years later – but she was superstitious, and a mention of one's real age might remind the Angel of Death that it was time to pay a visit. That superstition was so strong that it skipped two generations: my seemingly rational father was very ambivalent about celebrations of his birthday, and he never called me on mine.

Fifty years after the 'comprehensive 1931 census' in Poland, I naively wanted to celebrate the 90th birthday of my Great-aunt Sarah in Miami. Of the twelve Blattberg siblings, only Great-aunt Sarah had survived the Holocaust, and I loved her dearly. So I called her daughter to ask when Great-aunt Sarah was born, since the exact date appeared to be shrouded in mystery. 'Shush, shush! You shouldn't ask such things,' her daughter replied, clearly upset – and that was the end of the celebration.

Papa was tall and handsome, with jet-black hair, a broad forehead and small but lively brown eyes that sparkled when he laughed with abandon – a rare occasion. He was not athletic, but he had an imposing presence and was always impeccably groomed. Women were attracted to him. He liked to meet with his friends at the comfortable Viennese-style cafés, where young people would congregate to chat and to read the newspapers that were speared onto long hanging rods.

I don't know where he met Mama but I doubt that it was in a café. Mama hated cafés, she hated chit-chat, and was constantly in motion. She was of medium height, a slim brunette with piercing yet gentle brown eyes, and her mother's prominent Slavic cheekbones. She liked sports, especially hiking and skiing; after all, she had spent her childhood running freely in the *podhale*, the foothills of the Tatry mountains. She would often drag Papa to the ski resort of Zakopane in the Tatry, where he would sit in the valley while she went off trekking with her friends to Morskie Oko or Dolina Pięciu Stawów, or skiing in her quaint woolen pants.

She also liked swimming and often took Papa to a beach on the banks of the Vistula just outside Kraków. While they were swimming there on a fine day shortly after their engagement, all of their clothes were stolen, as well as Papa's wallet and the traditional gold watch of the prospective bridegroom that he had received from his future in-laws. The newly betrothed must have been quite a sight walking back to the city clad only in their swimsuits, with the beautiful engagement watch gone.

A bachelor living in Kraków on his own, Papa was frequently invited to dinner at the Schreibers, to be properly fed as befitted the future bridegroom in a nice Jewish family. He was very fond of apples, which Grandmother Schreiber always brought out for him along with the traditional after-dinner fruit. As Papa ate very little meat, and never touched anything that had some sauce on it or looked too rich, he consumed prodigious quantities of after-dinner apples, to Mama's acute embarrassment. He was quartering and peeling his second or third apple one evening, when he suddenly doubled over with pain. Grandmother blamed the apples – 'He ate too many, and perhaps they were too green' – and made Papa lie down with a hot-water-bottle. But it turned out that he had a burst appendix. It was before the age of antibiotics and Papa nearly died of peritonitis. The wedding was postponed for many months, until late May of 1933, while Papa slowly regained his strength. Grandma Estera Erna was convinced that she had caused his appendix to burst with her hot-water-bottle, and the fear of heating pads applied to stomach aches of unknown origin has been passed down to me over the decades.

After their wedding, my parents moved to an apartment on Aleja Krasinskiego, a broad avenue in a new and mostly Polish part of the city. The houses had all the modern conveniences, such as central heating. Mama had a live-in maid, a Polish countrywoman called Jadzia, who slept in a tiny room at the back of the kitchen. Papa worked with his Uncle Szymek Landau, who specialized in imports of fine textiles, mostly wool from England and exquisite cotton fabrics from Switzerland. He made a good living and, when I was born in January of 1937, a German nanny was hired to look after me because German nannies were considered the best. She raised me with appropriate Prussian discipline until, like all German nationals, she was expelled from Poland in late 1938.

No one appears to have noticed that Hitler was next door getting ready to wage war on the Jews. Mama was filling her pantry with jams and preserves from the summer bounty. Nothing bad was ever going to happen. It was like dancing on *The Titanic*, yet the passengers on *The Titanic* had the excuse of ignorance, whereas in our case everything was perfectly obvious: the rape of Czechoslovakia, the Anschluss in Austria, the rumblings of war, the Nazis' anti-Jewish insanity and the ever increasing Polish antisemitism.

3   *Lwów*

Oh, how I begged you to stay with us!
> (From one of Grandmother Laura's postcards.)

Mama was still making home-made jams and preserves to store in her pantry when the Germans invaded Poland on the first day of September 1939, crushing the western half of the country in a giant pincer which closed simultaneously from the west, the south and the north. Kraków was occupied within a matter of days. Abandoning everything in perfect order in Mama's immaculate apartment, we fled east to Mielec, just ahead of the German advance.

Papa, a footsoldier in the low-priority reserves, had already registered with the military authorities in Kraków about two weeks before the invasion. He registered again in Mielec, on September 4 (we still have this document, duly signed and stamped). Amidst the chaos of a total rout, he was not called for duty. Instead, Mama 'threw him out of the house', and made him join a group of Jewish men escaping to the east, while rumors about the Germans selecting men for cannon-fodder – human shields on the frontlines – were spreading like wildfire. These rumors were mostly based on Hitler's declaration of war speech, in which he was reported to have said that he would not wage war on women and children, and this was taken to mean that he would indeed 'wage war on men'.

As a result of Hitler's speech, young men, Poles and Jews alike, were choking the roads heading east, while all around them their unfortunate homeland was collapsing like a house of cards, despite pockets of gallant resistance. This exodus continued even after the Soviets invaded the eastern half of Poland on September 17. From Warsaw alone, more than 100,000 fled when the military issued an order for all able-bodied men to leave the capital when it was about to surrender.

Like almost everyone else, Papa set out into the unknown with little more than the clothes on his back, and no idea of where he was going. The only clear goal was to go far enough east to avoid becoming cannon-fodder. Although Mielec was substantially east of Kraków, it was still well within the western half of Poland that the Germans had allocated to themselves under the terms of the Soviet–German non-aggression pact, which had been signed barely a week before the invasion.

My parents decided that Papa would walk to the eastern area that was to be controlled by the Russians. He was going on foot because trains had stopped running and every automobile had been commandeered by the military. He was to remain in the east until the dust would settle and then come back to us in Mielec, where there would be plenty of food and produce from the farm at Gliny Wielkie. Meanwhile, Mama and I would be safe in Mielec with Grandfather Leib and Grandmother Laura, for Hitler would 'not wage war on women and children'.

This cockeyed plan was hatched during the days of insane panic that followed the German invasion, but Mama's head soon began to clear. She may have been a model, traditional *Hausfrau*, completely dependent on her husband for financial support, yet she was not one to await passively her destiny. I owe my life to her extraordinary decision to leave Mielec – a woman alone with a small child. Even before the atrocities of September 13 – the 'Erev Rosh Hashana massacre' in Mielec – Mama concluded that she was not going to stay under the Germans. She desperately tried to convince Grandfather and Grandmother Blattberg to go east with us, that we would manage somehow. My grandparents just as desperately tried to convince her to stay with them in Mielec, where Papa was 'bound to find his way back in a few weeks, where there was ample food and produce from the *dwór* at Gliny'. They themselves could not even think of leaving. As the oldest of the Blattberg clan, Grandfather Leib felt obliged to take care of his mother and of the family business. Great-grandmother Chava was living in her apartment in the family house at Rynek 17, and she would not budge from the home where she had raised twelve children. Besides, she had seen armies come and go before. It was not her first war, nor even her second, and furthermore the Germans would not stoop to harming an old woman such as herself.

Mama was just as adamant. She refused to stay under the Germans. She would head for Lwów, she would somehow find Papa on the road, she would find him! My grandparents bowed to the inevitable. A sturdy wagon drawn by two horses was brought in from Gliny and stocked with food, blankets and other necessities. A good friend, Moniek Gross, and two others who were also fleeing east came with us, to help Mama in exchange for the opportunity to ride in a wagon instead of walking.

Grandmother Laura was sure that we were going to our destruction. She threw herself on Mama and tried to pull her off the wagon, screaming '*Ja was więcej nigdy nie zobacze!*' [I shall never see you again!] Mama told me many times that she would forever see before her eyes that image of Grandmother Laura, and she blamed herself for not being able to convince my grandparents to leave Mielec.

The weather was radiant, one of the most beautiful Septembers in living memory. People, carts, and wagons were clogging the roads – deserters, disbanded groups of soldiers, thousands upon thousands of civilian refugees running to the east, toward the lesser Soviet evil. German fighter pilots amused themselves by swooping down very low, so low Mama said 'that you could see the whites of their eyes', to machine-gun the fleeing civilians. As soon as the whine of an approaching Stuka was heard, everyone would run for the fields or dive into ditches, or cower under their wagons if time was too short to hide. After one of the men in our small group had a buttock blown off while we were all lying huddled together, face down in a ditch, we decided to travel only by night and to hide in the woods by day.

Mama was constantly looking for Papa and obsessively scrutinizing the silhouette of every man we saw at a distance. As the days went by and none of the bedraggled, exhausted men along the country roads or in the village squares turned out to be Papa, she began to lose hope. She regretted her rash decision to leave Mielec. What if Papa was making his way back there at this very moment, on some other country road? What if we were never to see him again?

The German–Soviet demarcation line ran through the middle of the San River. The crossing was a harrowing experience. Once inside the Soviet zone, we resumed traveling by day. One afternoon, I began to scream *'Tatko, Tatko!'* [Daddy! Daddy!] as we were approaching a dejected group of men sitting at the foot of a village fountain. Mama was too despondent to even look in their direction and she didn't notice Papa in that unshaven, hungry bunch. He, of course, was not expecting to see us on the road. Desperately worried about us, he was heading west to Mielec and had stopped to rest for a while. We were already past the fountain – it was too late! – but I continued to scream 'Tatko! Tatko!' and tried to jump off the wagon, thus jolting Mama out of her stupor.

In the great game of 'What If?' that can be played at every critical junction of my childhood, that chance encounter in a dusty Ukrainian village plays a pivotal role. What if I had *not* persisted in screaming 'Tatko! Tatko!' and my parents had continued on their separate ways?

My father would have crossed back into the German zone while the demarcation line was still open and he would have perished with his family in Mielec. As for Mama and me, there were many branches open on our potential road. Would we have been deported to the Soviet Union, and would we have survived there – a woman alone with a small child? Would we have stayed in Lwów until the German invasion of June 1941 and then perished in the crematoria of Belzec, or elsewhere?

Or would Mama, unable to withstand the separation from her husband, have made yet another rash decision and applied for permission to return to the German zone, now renamed Generalgouvernement? This would have happened in early 1940, in one of the most Dantesque and least-documented scenes of the Jewish inferno. It would have happened like this: Mama would have stood in a very long line of Jewish refugees applying to the Germans – yes, to them – for permission to return to the Generalgouvernement.[1] The German officers would have been in Lwów, and other cities occupied by the Russians, as members of the 'Soviet–German

Resettlement Commissions' that were set up under the terms of a secret protocol in the German-Soviet non-aggression pact of August 1939. Under the terms of this protocol, Molotov and Ribbentrop had agreed to cooperate in an exchange of their respective nationals. The Germans were interested in recovering their ethnic Germans, and ended up with thousands upon thousands of Jewish refugees clamoring for permission to return to their hometowns.

In his monograph *The Horrible Decade*,[2] the historian Jan Tomasz Gross quotes from the memoir of a survivor:

> During the time of registration [with the Resettlement Commission], after standing in line for hours, I finally received a travel permit, which was then considered as a great stroke of good luck. One of the German officers addressed the waiting crowd and asked them: 'Jews, where are you going? Don't you know that we are going to kill you?'

And Jan Gross also quotes from the memoirs of Nikita Khruschev, who was then the First Secretary of the Communist Party in Ukraine. Khruschev tells of his amazement at seeing throngs of Jews waiting in line and bribing Gestapo agents for permission to return to Poland. Everyone, it seems, knew that the Jews were doomed – except the Jews themselves.

But, unlike countless others who were less fortunate, we were reunited by the fountain in that dusty Ukrainian village. We found refuge in Lwów, where the Beck family, our relatives by marriage, took us into their home. Aunt Binka, the wife of Papa's Uncle Szymek Landau, was a Beck from Lwów. Many relatives and friends from Kraków arrived after us. Grandmother Schreiber, Uncle Menek and his young wife Hela, Aunt Janka and her husband Jules Wassertheil and my cousin Romek staggered in. Aunt Herminka and my cousins Marcel and Anita, who had been trapped in Poland just as they were about to leave for Buenos Aires to join Uncle Lonek, also ended up in Lwów. Grandmother Schreiber tried frantically to 'keep the family together' and, after Mama and I left Mielec, the remaining three Schreiber siblings followed us to Lwów.

The three Schiff brothers, Zelek, Kalmek and David (Duduś), Mama's first cousins from Tarnów, straggled in with their sister's fiancé. Their parents had thrown them out of the house ahead of the German advance, just as Mama had done with Papa. The elder Schiffs kept their daughter, Guscia, and Zelek's young bride, Hela, with them in Tarnów 'because the Germans wouldn't harm women and old men'.

The Soviets were overwhelmed by the hundreds of thousands of refugees, Poles and Jews alike, who presented them with a monumental political headache and who were straining the already meager resources of eastern Poland, now annexed to the Soviet Union and incorporated into the Soviet Republics of Ukraine and Belorussia. There was no question of setting up a relief agency to provide food and shelter, as is the case with modern-day refugees: *'Nie rabotayesh nie kushayesh'* [If you don't work you don't eat] was much more than an official party slogan. It was a grim reality.

The very concept of 'refugees' – foreigners granted temporary refuge on Soviet soil – was alien to the Soviet mind. The Russian language itself was revealing. We were called *'biezhency'*, a word which means 'those who have run away', as if we had committed a crime by escaping from the Germans and could not be trusted.

There were no official displays of antisemitism. Rather, the Russians engaged in their own form of madness, a reflexive distrust of anything foreign, especially if it was 'Western'.

Perhaps nothing illustrates this peculiarly Russian paranoia more vividly than the tragic story of some of the Jewish wretches from the 'Lublinland Reservation'. This was a stretch of desolate countryside in the Lublin area that the Germans had set up shortly after the invasion as a dumping ground for rural Jews who had just been expelled from hundreds of small communities. During the months of November and December 1939, the Germans – who had not yet finalized their approach to the 'final solution' – kept driving Jews from this reservation into the Soviet Union. Their *modus operandi* was fiendishly simple: the Jews were pushed into the rivers which formed the border between the German and the Soviet zone and SS sharpshooters posted on the riverbanks kept shooting at those who did not drown. To complete the circles of hell, survivors who had managed to swim across the river were immediately arrested by Soviet border guards posted on the other side and, accused of 'spying', they were deported for 're-education' into some of the harshest gulags, where the mortality rate was extremely high.

Soviet citizenship was imposed on the indigenous population in the entire occupied area in November of 1939. The refugees were given the choice between retaining Polish citizenship or accepting a Soviet passport (it was the so-called *passportizatsya* or 'passportization'). It was a difficult decision, as everyone was aware of the deportations to labor camps deep inside the Soviet Union that most likely awaited those who refused to be 'passportized'.

'Resettlement' to labor camps began in November, not only because all foreigners were automatically suspected of being spies but also because the authorities were overwhelmed with the numbers of refugees who continued to arrive despite the Soviet efforts to push them back at the border. Deeply embedded within the Russian psyche is the concept of the individual citizen as an indentured servant of the state, and resettling of entire populations to suit the state's convenience was a solution that came naturally to the mind of Soviet bureaucrats. It was done routinely within the Soviet Union itself and we now had to accommodate ourselves to that system.

Lwów was a large, ethnically mixed city, populated by mutually hostile Ukrainians, Poles and Jews, with other groups sprinkled into the cauldron for good measure. Polish antisemitism had been particularly violent there but overt anti-Jewish activities, and even use of the derogatory '*Zhyd*', were forbidden by the Soviets, who kept themselves very busy persecuting 'spies', 'enemies of the people', 'anti-Soviet elements' and 'bourgeois capitalists'.

The Becks were stripped of their property, which included a suite of offices located near the university. However, the former caretaker's apartment, two rooms with kitchen and bath, had somehow been overlooked by the Russian authorities. This administrative oversight provided us with a stroke of extraordinary good fortune, a decent place to live at a time when housing conditions were dreadful. Mrs Beck came running one morning during the expropriation. 'Quick! Quick,' she shouted, 'let's move you into the caretaker's place before they take it away!'

We were extremely lucky. Most of the refugees around us lived in makeshift quarters or were packed into rooms without kitchen privileges. They generally rented such rooms from Lwów residents who owned a living area significantly larger than deemed necessary by the Soviets and who were terrified of having their homes requisitioned for 'communal apartments'.

Our apartment became a gathering place, especially the kitchen where crowds of women took turns cooking whatever food was at hand. The men would gather in the evening to engage in palavering about the course of events and the 'passportization' issue.

It was a difficult time, with anxiety about the 'passportization' decision and anguish about the fate of our loved ones left behind in the Generalgouvernement adding to material hardships. Notwithstanding massive round-ups and deportations of Polish nationals, those who were opposed to 'passportization' argued that Soviet citizens were also at risk of deportation or imprisonment. Moreover, they were never allowed to travel abroad. Should we accept a Soviet passport, we might be forced to spend the rest of our lives inside the vast prison that was Russia, even after the end of the war – a prospect so terrifying that my parents decided to retain their Polish citizenship, fully aware that we would most likely be deported.

Mama's two sisters and the Schiff 'boys' – Zelek, Kalmek and Duduś, the sons of Grandmother Erna's sister Sarah – remained Polish as well. Only Uncle Menek, his wife Hela, and Grandmother Erna opted for Soviet citizenship.

Life settled down into a sort of routine. Papa was working. I had a proper crib. Mama always tried to provide a quiet corner for me. She constantly read books to me and I memorized vast quantities of poems and nursery rhymes. It seems that I knew by heart most of Tuwim's poems for children, but the only one I still remember is a verse about a locomotive standing at the station on a very hot day, spewing steam, while three very fat men sat inside the train, eating very fat sausages. I later carried the image of those sausages with me to Russia, where there were none to be found, and I eat sausage as a comfort food even now.

There were very few children of my age within our circle. My cousin Romek was more than two years older than me – a huge difference because I was not yet three. My cousins Marcel and Anita were about eight and eleven. I played occasionally with three-year-old Henryś Maj, the son of refugee friends from Kraków, but for the most part I was left to my own devices, wandering among crowds of adult legs with my doll Falunia, a stuffed rabbit called Pufciu Cylinder, and my books.

I am sure that I did not know how to read at the time of the 'passportization' crisis, but several people told me that I did, probably because I knew all my books by heart. One of my favorites was *Zosia Sierota* [Zosia the Orphan Girl], the story of a girl who had lost her parents. I was 'reading' it one day when someone inadvertently collided with me and sent me sprawling on the kitchen floor. I burst into tears. Mama took me on her knee and tried to console me, saying, '*Biedna Ritusia, szwęda się wszystkim pod nogami*' [Poor little Ritusia wandering underfoot everywhere].

'I am not poor,' I sobbed in indignation. 'Zosia Sierota is poor, but I am not poor because I have a mommy and a daddy!'

And indeed, for the remainder of the war and during the dreadful time of postwar Poland, I always considered myself as someone privileged, never 'poor', because I felt always sheltered by my parents' love. This is their greatest gift to me, and for this I am forever grateful.

4 Kuma

Where is this place located, in what 'gubernia'?
(From one of Great-aunt Gusta's postcards.)

Although deportations continued in successive waves, we were spared for several months, despite our refusal of Soviet citizenship. No doubt my parents spent many sleepless nights, expecting to hear the sound of boots on the stairs because the NKVD[1] men almost always came in the middle of the night. By June of 1940, we had something else to worry about, as we engaged in 'anti-Soviet activity' by hiding Mama's cousins – the three Schiff brothers and their sister's sweetheart – in the attic above our apartment. The four young men had good reason to fear the NKVD: as *cholostoi*, single men without dependants, they would be taken to the harshest camps and worked mercilessly. Two other Schiff relatives had already died there.

They came for us a little before daybreak in late June. Papa was accused of *spekulatsya* (black-marketeering), a rather hilarious charge against a man who was scared of everything, 'even his own shadow', and wouldn't have lasted a day wheeling and dealing on the black market. It seems that someone – and now that I have read her postcards I think it was Grandmother Blattberg – had arranged for too many goods to be shipped to us from Kraków: blankets, warm clothes, some fabrics and enough children's shoes to 'take me into my tenth year', an overabundance that must have led the authorities to suspect my father of *spekulatsya*.

The NKVD men ordered that all of our possessions, and not just the products of *spekulatsya*, be confiscated. But Mama, who was a fighter, managed to reclaim a few things, including a folding crib which traveled with us to Russia. The rest they took away: our blankets, our pillows, even our soap. We waited at the NKVD registration center until 2 a.m. the following day to be processed for 'resettlement', and then were taken to the railway station, without anything to eat or drink. Ukrainian soldiers dumped us and our belongings into a cattle-truck that stood on a side-track, one of many cars about to form an *eshalon*, a very long train used for conveying deportees. There were already many people in the car and we were the last ones to be squeezed in before the doors were locked.

As the dawn light filtered through the minuscule windows, the inmates counted heads – 27 adults and two children – and they reapportioned the floor space to accommodate everyone as far as possible. We had enough room for my folding crib and for my parents to sit with their legs outstretched. No one knew where we were going, nor when the train would leave, because *eshalons* were often shunted to the side for a long time.

We could hear people running outside along the track, shouting for their loved ones. Although this kind of display was forbidden, the armed soldiers who were patrolling the length of the train on either side were letting some people through, while pushing others back with the butts of their rifles and swearing at them in Ukrainian. My babysitter, Basia Beck, and Papa's cousin Hela Landau managed to find us and they handed us some food and water through the closely spaced steel bars on the tiny window. Grandmother Schreiber arrived, almost beside herself with grief, and proceeded to spill most of the water that she had brought us. Between bouts of sobbing, she told us that Aunt Herminka and her two children were already on their way to some unknown destination, while the Wassertheils – Aunt Janka, Uncle Jules and Romeczek – were locked inside one of the many cars of our *eshalon*. The three Schreiber sisters had been engulfed in one single night by the same giant wave of deportations. Grandmother, Uncle Menek and Aunt Hela, who had accepted 'passportization' in early 1940, were protected by their Soviet citizenship, at least for the time being.

Meanwhile, unbeknown to us, the three Schiff brothers and their sister's fiancé were also locked inside our *eshalon*. They had heard the commotion in our apartment on the night of the NKVD raid and understood that we were taken. Since they were completely dependent on the family for their survival, continuing to hide in our attic no longer made any sense. They waited until morning and then left. Unshaven and bedraggled, they were stopped by the first policeman who saw them in the street. The man was decent enough to let them collect their things before escorting them to the NKVD station. They sat in the processing room for hours. David, the youngest brother (whom everyone called Duduś) was observing the registration clerk: paperwork for families was placed on the right side of his desk; paperwork for singles on the left. When their turn came, he persuaded his brothers to let him register first. As expected, the clerk placed his paperwork onto the left-side pile, but Duduś, with his broken Russian and much sign language, tried to explain that he, his two brothers and their sister's fiancé should be considered as a 'family unit'.

The clerk was unconvinced. 'What's all this fuss about? You are all going to Poltava anyway,' he joked. Of course, they all knew that they were not going to Poltava, a Ukrainian city relatively close to Lwów, but much, much further into the depths of Russia.

Duduś requested to see the *natchialnik*, the headman. The *natchialnik*, an NKVD captain, a tall handsome man from the Caucasus, agreed to make them a 'family unit', after some additional haggling. 'I need your signature, comrade captain,' the clerk said. Duduś quickly handed his gold fountain pen to the captain, who signed them over to the 'family unit' pile, and kept the pen – a favor for a favor, and what a favor it was, for they would have probably died in the gulag for *cholostoi*.

We stood in the station sidings for two days, without receiving food or water. The car was like a baking oven, people were gasping for breath in the searing heat and retching from the nauseating stench that emanated from the 'toilet' – a hole in the floor in a corner. We began to move on the third day, but soon lurched to a stop at an isolated station in the countryside, where we were given water, bread and a pail of something that looked like soup. Two days later, again spent without food or water, we were shunted to a dead-end track somewhere beyond Kiev. This time they fed us potatoes and allowed women with small children to climb down for some fresh air.

'There was a family called Blat in the car next to ours,' Mama told us. 'Mr Blat was very ill and he was gasping for air in the cattle car, so his wife persuaded him to go outside with their children. A guard started swearing at him in Ukrainian and hit him on the head with his rifle-butt. The poor man dropped dead on the spot. They hit me too, because I was straying, in the ribs, so hard that I was in agony for days.'

Mama saw a dead body being removed from a neighboring car and then we continued to roll, frequently halting on side-tracks in order to make way for more important traffic.

There were no sanitary facilities. Men and women would take turns going to the 'toilet', a couple of women holding a blanket for privacy around a woman, and the men doing the same for a man. Papa could not bring himself to defecate in public and after about a week his abdomen became stiff, his face turned blue. Mama thought that he was going to die, but someone saved the day by forcing him to submit to a makeshift enema.

As we moved deeper and deeper into the Russian heartland and the likelihood of escape decreased, the guards relaxed their vigilance; men were allowed outside during halts and deportees from different cars were allowed to mingle. Whenever the train would stop at a real station, one or two people from each car would queue up for *kipiatok*, boiling water from a giant samovar, while others went to fetch pails of cold water. One day the train started to move while Papa was still drawing water from a pump, but luckily he managed to jump into the last car before it was too late.

Sometime in late July we stopped by a lake which was completely surrounded by seemingly virgin forest. From there, we were transported to a camp, a *specposiolek* [special settlement[2]] that was to be our home for the next thirteen months. It was a forest settlement called *lesoutchiastok Kuma*. Coined by the Soviet penal system, the word *lesoutchiastok* means 'a parcel of land within the forest', and Kuma was exactly that, a labor camp engulfed within a wilderness of primordial forest and malarial swamps. Lest the mention of 'camp' evoke the dreadful gulag imagery, let me hasten to mention that Kuma was a camp where families were kept together and mothers of small children were exempt from heavy work, however harsh our treatment, however backbreaking the labor of the men. But we did not know that when we were first assembled before the camp commander, a Mari by the name of Saratov, who always had a huge German shepherd by his side.

The camp was a collection of wooden barracks set in a clearing. We and the Wassertheils were assigned to Barracks 50, a small hut at the periphery of the camp, right by the forest edge. The Schiff boys were first placed in a huge unheated dormitory called *obshcie zhytie* [communal living], though later they were allowed to move in with us to form a 'family unit'. Our hut was locked at night, but during the day we could roam freely. Even if we had a map, it would have been of no use because the Soviets treated the location of camps as a state secret, not to be revealed on any map. Nor would there be any point in trying to escape for we were truly in the middle of nowhere, deep within an endless maze of forest, swamp, lakes and rivers – the many tributaries of the giant Volga and Kama Rivers. Even by Russian standards, Mariyskaya ASSR (the Mari Autonomous Soviet Socialist Republic) was a godforsaken place, with a sparse population composed mostly of Maris: a short and stocky people of Mongolian descent.

Every able-bodied inmate was assigned to work, though those who were truly sick, like Uncle Wassertheil, were exempted from heavy labor. The men were clearing the swamps and the forest in order to help make the area less of a hellhole. They felled the giant trees with axes and handsaws and removed the bark with a tool that was shaped like a huge fork. Fir trees often reached a height of 20 or 30 meters. These enormous trunks were transported by means of a backbreaking contraption to a nearby river, a tributary of the Volga. They were dumped into the water and allowed to float downstream to a collection point on the Volga. The river froze in winter, entombing the logs within the thick ice. Spring thaw began when the ice cracked with a mighty roar, as loud as thunder, and the logs were freed from hibernation.

Papa was among the men assigned to the task of forest-clearing. He was not much of a woodsman but he managed somehow and was not singled out for punishment. Work began with the sound of a gong at precisely 6 a.m. Tardiness was severely punished. The first offense resulted in a warning and a 25 per cent reduction in wages. Yes, the inmates were paid. The wages were symbolic but the symbolism indicated that we were in a labor camp and not in a penal colony (gulag). The second warning came with a mandatory sentence of six months in jail for being even five minutes late.

Any jail sentence was preceded by a 'trial'. Duduś tells of witnessing the trial of a young man who had reported for work late, albeit with a note from the camp nurse to prove that he was ill. A judge from the local district was presiding and the young man, acting as his own lawyer, attempted to exculpate himself with a long, fiery speech. When the young man shut up after handing in the paper from the nurse, the judge asked him, 'Have you finished?'

'Yes, citizen judge,' answered the young man.

'Six months,' said the judge, and got up.

The young man was taken away to serve his sentence and that was the end of the trial. The judge then took an ear-trumpet from his briefcase, brought it to his ear and exchanged a few words with Saratov, the camp commander. The magistrate was stone deaf and had not heard a word of the young man's pleading!

While the deaf judge dealt with the lesser offenses, the more serious infractions, such as 'anti-Soviet activities', fell within the purview of the NKVD. Duduś recalled for us one such incident, which occurred while he was waiting in line to collect his bread ration. A forestry engineer from Warsaw, by the name of Oppenheimer, was standing ahead of Duduś and still further up the line was a young woman with a child in her arms. All of a sudden, a militiaman pulled the young woman from the ranks and threw her on the ground, with the child still in her arms. Oppenheimer, unable to contain himself, hit the militiaman with his fist. Nothing happened that day, but the next morning two NKVD soldiers took Oppenheimer away to an undisclosed destination. A week later his wife was notified that her husband, a young and healthy man, had unexpectedly died of 'pneumonia'.

We were all fortunate inasmuch as Saratov was a decent and intelligent man who did not particularly relish meting out punishment. Thus Duduś and his brothers were able to escape penalty for an offense that, according to the rules, should have sent them straight into the clutches of the NKVD. This incident happened on Yom Kippur of 1940. Although the majority of Kuma inmates were Jewish, Yom Kippur was an ordinary work day since public worship was forbidden, as was the display of religious artifacts such as a prayer shawl. However, the Schiff brothers, who came from an Orthodox family, took the risk of skipping work in order to form an improvised congregation along with some 50 other men. Zelek even removed his prayer shawl from its hiding-place.

As they were all swaying and chanting, Saratov appeared, flanked by his ever-present German shepherd. The commander was enraged. He could plainly see that they were praying – an anti-Soviet activity – but he chose to ignore that particular offense, concentrating instead on their failure to report for work.

'*Zabastovka*!' [Strike!] he screamed. 'Don't you know that it is forbidden to strike?' They were all petrified because attempts at *zabastovka* were among the most severely repressed offenses. Luckily for them, Saratov was not all that keen on jeopardizing his production quota by sending to jail, or worse, a large number of some of his most productive workers. Instead, they were all docked a portion of their wages and made to report for work 'on the double'. For this group of observant Jews, however, being forced to desecrate the Day of Atonement was punishment enough.

People went to jail for all sorts of reasons, so much so that *tiurma* [jail] was one of the first Russian words that I learned. We children played a game called *tiurma*, which basically consisted of picking a victim to be sentenced to 'sit' (a word which in Russian also means 'serving a prison sentence'). My first conscious memory, the first one that I am sure is my own, is of refusing to come to lunch when called because I had not finished 'sitting'. The youngest child in my small group, and the only girl, I 'sat' a great deal.

Considering the harsh conditions in the camp, one might be tempted to think that 'sitting' was not such a disaster, but unfortunately people died in jail rather often, usually from malnutrition. The phrase '*Nie rabotayesh nie kuszayesh*' [If you don't work you don't eat], the unofficial motto of the Soviet Union, revealed its full meaning inside the jail.

And even in the camp a worker's daily ration was determined by his productivity. As '*stakhanovists*' [high-output workers] Duduś and his brothers were each entitled to 2 kg of bread daily, while Papa's output entitled him to only 0.5 kg. Mama and I also received 0.5 kg of bread each. The bread looked like a brick, it had the density of a brick, and it tasted like clay. Two meals a day were served at the canteen. The staple food was *lapsha*, wide noodles made from a dark flour and floating in a watery broth. Luckily, we were able to supplement our rations to some degree by bartering in the underground economy. People who received packages from home or who had brought with them tradeable goods – pants, sweaters, wool for knitting and the like – engaged in lively barter with the neighboring villagers. We had almost nothing to barter because the NKVD soldiers who came to arrest us in Lwów had confiscated practically everything we owned. Mama and Papa were constantly hungry but, thanks to the parcels that we received sporadically from Uncle Menek and my two grandmothers, Romeczek and I were reasonably well fed. We even had butter and honey once in a while. I cannot do justice to the role that parcels from our family played in our survival without a discussion of my grandmothers' postcards, and I shall come back to the subject of what we ate and wore, and to the price of a single egg or a glass of milk, as this story unfolds.

Mosquitoes were a scourge, as were the *barachatch* – tiny gnats resembling the 'no-se'ems' we have in the north-east, but much more vicious. One breathed them in through the mouth and the nose; they bit eyes and ears. Processions of strangely dressed inmates would emerge from the barracks at dawn, trudging to work with every inch of their bodies covered, with scraps of fabric and improvised netting shrouding their heads, like demented beekeepers. Some men wore their wives' hats, the kind of dainty prewar things that had veils in front. Nothing helped.

Soon after our arrival to Kuma, Mama was stricken with malaria, a disease that was endemic to the area, as was a form of encephalitis which was also borne by mosquitoes. Her malaria attacks were terrifying to watch, and I am just as glad that I don't really remember them. Duduś, however, still speaks to this day of Mama's hollow-eyed stare and convulsive shuddering: 'Those shivers, those dreadful shivers, it was something horrifying.'

At first, Duduś and his brothers lived in a barracks with a large group of men. Some of them would sing in the evening to stave off hunger pangs.

'What do Jews do when they are hungry?' Duduś asked us rhetorically when we tape-recorded his testimony.

'They sing,' he replied, answering his own question.

We Blattbergs must be an exception to this rule because not one of us can sing. The Schiffs, on the other hand, are all quite gifted. Duduś, who is a born leader and who has a nice, strong baritone, was conducting occasional singing sessions after work. One night, they noticed that Saratov was standing by the door, completely mesmerized by their singing. Saratov, a lover of music stranded in that wilderness, ordered a very reluctant Duduś to organize a camp-wide choir and to prepare for a concert. There were many Jews in the camp but there were also Poles, as well as people of other nationalities, and in that Tower of Babel they sang in Yiddish, Polish and Russian, and even in German. Saratov never missed a rehearsal and always listened with a beatific smile on his face. Membership of the choir soon became a coveted privilege as it provided some degree of protection from the harsh discipline of the camp. Thus, despite being repeatedly late for work, Zelek was not punished, protected by his beautiful voice.

Among the inmates there was a Polish count, the real thing, a man who under normal circumstances would never address a Jew as 'Mr'. This count had a young and beautiful second wife and a seventeen-year-old daughter who was a professionally trained soprano. Counts didn't fare well under the Soviets and that one came begging Duduś to accept his daughter into the choir, in order to improve her lot.

'Sir, you understand that I wasn't born a cobbler (a reference to his troubles as a former aristocrat)...yes Sir...of course Sir...quite so, Sir.'

It was a pleasure to hear, and the daughter was a valuable addition to the choir. She readily learned to sing Yiddish songs. Saratov was so pleased that he decreed the troupe would go on a concert tour of the area as soon as possible.

Almost a year passed. Papa was transferred to a less strenuous 'office job'. Duduś had an easy job as a carpenter in charge of making axe handles from birch wood. Once he had mastered the skills required to make a proper axe handle, Duduś was able to fulfill his daily production quota in a few hours and he spent a portion of every day writing poetry.

The first full-scale concert performance to be held outside the camp was scheduled for Sunday, June 22, 1941. At daybreak on that same Sunday, the Germans invaded the Soviet Union, taking the Soviets completely by surprise and inflicting enormous losses on them. Such was Saratov's obsession with his choir that the concert took place as scheduled, with Duduś as the conductor. However, as a sign of everyone's patriotism, the three German songs that were to be part of the program were eliminated.

Although Saratov's dream of a concert tour was shattered, the one and only outside performance was a huge success. Afterward, a Mari from a nearby village said to Duduś, '*Eto bylo vielikolepno, no niekulturno*' [It was absolutely magnificent, but you have no manners].

'What do you mean? I don't understand,' Duduś asked.

'*Eto bylo vielikolepno, no niekulturno*,' the man repeated, and added irritably, 'And why was your back turned to the audience?'

Darkness descended on our loved ones in Mielec and in Lwów. We were instantly cut off from our family in Poland as if they had all been sucked into a black hole. Lwów, once again renamed Lemberg, became the headquarters for the fifth district of the Generalgouvernement. Grandmother Schreiber, Uncle Menek, and Aunt Hela were trapped under the Germans.

The Polish government-in-exile in London was now an ally of the Soviets and General Sikorski, its leader, negotiated with Stalin an 'amnesty' agreement for the Polish citizens who had been forcibly taken to the Soviet Union – people like ourselves.

We were set free in early August and were given permission to settle anywhere, except in large cities and 'forbidden zones', numerous areas which were off-limits to foreigners.

Meanwhile the Germans were advancing east, deep into Russia. Death and devastation on an unprecedented scale followed in their wake. We decided to go as far away from the Germans as we could, to Kazakhstan in Central Asia. Aunt Herminka was already there with my cousins Marcel and Anita. Kazakhstan was assumed to be beyond the reach of the Germans. Once there, one could even dream of 'sneaking' into Persia, perhaps of reaching Palestine. Young men were also hoping to join the Anders Army, the Polish army that was forming in Central Asia under the Sikorski–Stalin agreement.

Our small group embarked on an epic journey to Astrakhan, a city in the Volga delta on the Caspian Sea, which was the gateway to Central Asia. We traveled mostly on the water, first along the Vetluga, and then on the Volga. We were going downstream in the flat open boats, rafts really, that were made famous by the 'Volga Boatmen' song. The journey took six weeks, of which I remember only the 'mosquito wars' between my cousin Romek and myself. Come dark, the mosquitoes attacked in vicious, noisy assault waves, thousands upon thousands hurtling down with the same buzzing whine as the Stukas that had so terrified me in September of 1939. They did not bite daintily, rather they fell like the blow of a fist. Romek and I would wake up screaming – 'He hit me!'; 'No, she hit me' – and we would end up having fist-fights in the night.

We were free but we had absolutely no resources. Yet we were not that much worse off than the millions of Russians who were fleeing before the German advance. Overnight, the price of food increased more than a hundredfold. A single egg now cost about as much as a skilled worker used to earn in Lwów in a whole month. Although the authorities were doing their best to evacuate civilians, there was chaos and hunger everywhere. Massive relocation of heavy industry to the Ural area was proceeding; entire factories, entire towns were transferred. Trucks, planes, munitions, armor of every kind began rolling off these new makeshift assembly lines. The scale of that effort and the rapidity of the deployment were unbelievable. We civilians were lost in this titanic move, but somehow we reached Astrakhan, where we were fed *lapsha* in a soup kitchen. Mama and I were placed in a shelter for women with small children, while Papa had to sleep outdoors.

Papa made but one single mention of this trip, astoundingly a year or two before his death in 1995. 'The Russians aren't bad people,' he said. 'They tried to provide shelter for women with small children.'

During our journey down the Volga, my parents befriended a Russian Jewish couple who were fleeing the German advance. These people convinced them that Mama, who had been devastated by malaria in the *uciastok* at Kuma and whose health was shaky, would not survive in the climate of Central Asia. The couple had relatives in the village of Kambarka, far away in the Udmurdskaya ASSR in the west-central Urals, not too far from a *pristan* (a boat dock) on a Kama tributary that was called the Kambarka River. They gave us a letter of introduction to their relatives and advised us to go to Kambarka where, they said, the climate would be better for Mama. We left our group of family and friends in Astrakhan and continued our journey alone. The Wassertheils and the Schiff 'boys' set out for Kazakhstan while we reversed course, navigating the Volga upstream until we joined the Kama and turned north-east toward the Urals.

Until this moment of writing I never really wondered about my parents' extraordinary decision to travel all alone for thousands of miles to a godforsaken place where they knew not a soul. Abandoning the support of family and friends, penniless in a war-torn country, barely speaking Russian, they set out into an unknown and primitive vastness. It amazes me that Papa, the *'bojsie Żyd'* [scaredy-cat Jew] afraid of his own shadow, could have been bold enough to make such a decision. He must have loved Mama very much. Papa will forever remain for me an enigma, a complex, emotionally crippled man, but one thing I now see with the clear vision of old age: my father was a *mentsh* in the fundamental sense of the word – a man who did his duty no matter what the cost.

We arrived at the *pristan* that was closest to the village of Kambarka late on a November afternoon. The river was still navigable, though it would soon freeze for the duration of the long winter. We were alone at the *pristan* as we set out to cross the forest that separated us from the village of Kambarka. It was snowing and we lost our way. We were wandering around in circles and did not realize that we had returned to the river bank at a spot where it formed a cliff some 20 meters high. The snow was blinding us and we were about to step off into the dark void below when 'Dziadziusio' (Little Grand-father) Schreiber come down from Heaven at the last moment. He guided Mama's feet and brought us back to the path that led to Kambarka.

Papa broke down and, saying that we were doomed, he refused to go any further. He sat down in the snow. I was very sick and delirious with fever, a heavy bundle in Mama's arms. Suddenly, there appeared many pairs of eyes glowing around us in the dark. We were encircled by a pack of wolves. After a while, the howling started as the hungry beasts were making ready to attack us.

Dziadziusio Schreiber performed another miracle and sent us a group of angels all dressed in white, with flowing white capes. The angels were moving through the forest in horse-driven sleighs. Mama spoke only broken Russian but she knew enough to point to me, crying, *'Rebionok bolnoi'* [The child is sick].

The Chief Angel took one look and said, *'Davai'* [Let's go]. Soon we were tucked in on a sleigh, together with our bundles, and we arrived in Kambarka on the wings of White Angels.

Many years later, as I was watching a movie on the war, it suddenly dawned on me that our angels must have been Siberian soldiers in their white camouflage, a detachment of the very same troups who saved Moscow a few weeks later, and whom the Wehrmacht cursed in their communiqués, calling them the 'White Devils'. And indeed, we were trapped in that forest at a desperate time for the Red Army, when reserve Siberian troops were being hastily brought in from the east while the Germans were approaching Moscow.

5 Kambarka

We arrived in Kambarka on a snowy November night in 1941. The White Angels who had saved us from the wolves and the forest brought us to the village in a horse-drawn sleigh, turned around and departed for the front. My parents were left standing all alone in the night with their bundles and a sick child who was struggling for breath. It turned out that I had developed pneumonia, but fortunately I managed to recover on my own – which was very clever of me since we had no antibiotics.

It was an episode that I recall only as a dark blanket of exhaustion and listlessness which kept smothering me for much of that first winter. To make matters worse, we were camping like nomads in the corner of various *izbas*, sometimes sleeping in a bed, sometimes on the floor. This happened because Kambarka was teeming with newcomers: mostly Soviet evacuees in their hundreds, but also recently freed Polish citizens like ourselves. Our village was fast transforming itself into a woefully overcrowded town where it was almost impossible to find housing and, having wasted precious months wandering downriver all the way to Astrakhan and then back upriver again, we were at a particular disadvantage as late-coming stragglers.

Civilians were left to fend for themselves as every available resource was devoted to the war effort. From north to south, the Urals formed the backbone of production for the military, thanks largely to the heroic evacuation of heavy equipment and factory personnel from the industrial areas that were now occupied by the Germans. The Udmurt ASSR, our own little corner of the Urals, was rich in mineral resources, including iron and oil. Kambarka itself had been founded in the eighteenth century as a settlement for the iron-making workers from a nearby smeltery. And oil, of course, was the life-blood of the war, the more so during the bleak years of 1942–43, while the Germans were threatening the major oil fields of the Caucasus. It is for this reason that our *Neftebaza* (petroleum base), a secret installation located on the shore of the Kambarka Lake, was the most important facility in the area, though with hindsight I am now wondering if 'petroleum' was really its only business. No doubt production of the deadly gas lewisite, that would later saddle the unsuspecting inhabitants of Kambarka with one of the world's biggest stockpiles of chemical weapons, had already begun while we were living there.

Though several people associated with the *Neftebaza* would later play an important role in our lives, my own little universe in the beginning extended only as far as the small block of houses in our immediate vicinity. My first clear recollection of that period is of living in a one-room *izba* with a local family of four. It was during an outbreak of trachoma, a nasty infection of the eyes that often leads to blindness and is extremely contagious upon simple contact. The two children of the house had hideously suppurating eyes and their eyelashes were growing into their eyeballs instead of pointing outward!

Mama's incessant hovering was driving me crazy. She was constantly yelling, 'Don't touch anything, for God's sake, don't rub your eyes!' She was forcing me to wear gloves indoors like a freak. I was not allowed to play outside in the cold on account of my recent pneumonia and I was not allowed to play with the two children. I had nothing to do but sit caged in our little corner of the room, staring at those terrifying eyes. On top of it all, I had a very painful bladder infection. To this day, I can still see myself sitting on my potty, crying bitterly because I had to pee but couldn't. Mama was sitting on the floor next to me, endlessly pouring water back and forth between a chipped enameled jug and a small washbasin, hoping that the tinkling sound would encourage me to pee. Silent tears were rolling down her cheeks while she kept pouring that water from the jug to the washbasin and back. It was the only time during my entire childhood that I saw Mama crying, and her tears terrified me even more than our roommates' inverted eyes.

Our luck changed for the better during the spring of 1942, when we moved to more spacious quarters, the front half of a long room in a three-storey wooden house on Karl Marx Street, Kambarka's main street. From the courtyard, four steps led down to our basement level entrance. Our half, the better half of the room, to the right of the door, drew some light from two tiny double-glazed windows, while on the opposite side a dusty curtain screened a sort of alcove that was always dark and gloomy even when the curtain was drawn open for the day. A tall, blond woman from Moscow lived behind that curtain with her ten-year-old son Volodya. We all shared a cast-iron stove which was used both for heating the room and cooking our meals.

Volodya was morose, pale and silent. He came and went like a ghost and I don't remember him laughing or playing with anyone. Every once in a while, Mama and Volodya's mother would sit down in the dark alcove and talk, their voices so hushed that I could not hear a thing. They would always stop their whispering if I approached. This did not surprise me, as I was already used to the strange, secretive ways of grown-ups. I did not know at the time that people were dreadfully afraid of their children, who often brought them trouble by repeating on the outside fragments of their parents' subversive conversations.

It was only years later, when we were safely out of Kambarka, that Mama told me our roommates' story. The blond woman from Moscow, with her long hair pinned in a thick coil on top of her head, was the widow of a Soviet diplomat who had been posted in Paris for many years. Upon their return to Moscow, he was immediately arrested and executed as a spy. According to the logic of Soviet paranoia, it was perfectly obvious that contact with the West had transformed the diplomat into a spy and an enemy of the people. His wife, too, was deemed contaminated and was banished from Moscow.

Volodya's mother worked for the same pitiful wages as almost everyone else in town. With the exception of a privileged few at the *Neftebaza*, who were paid real wages and ate real food, none could survive on wages alone. Some, unable to sustain the constant struggle, died of starvation, but most people somehow managed to fend for themselves in the underground economy, by performing an intricate ballet called 'wheeling around'. The steps of 'wheeling around' depended on one's skills and position, but the theme never varied. It was always about the search for 'access', the right connections in the right places. Survival was predicated on having things done *po blatu* [an untranslatable Russian phrase meaning 'having things done by means of a connection'].

Volodya's mother was less successful than most, perhaps because her internal passport revealed her politically 'untrustworthy' status and made people wary of associating with her. Volodya and his mother were always hungry. I vividly remember what happened on a winter afternoon when the mother unexpectedly brought home a jar of honey. Instead of putting it away and doling it out carefully, they immediately devoured their honey all at once, as if afraid that some invisible hand would snatch it from them. In their haste, they did not even bother to draw their curtain and, sitting on my parents' bed, I could see everything they were doing. After sopping up some of the golden liquid with small crusts of bread, they switched to lapping it up from a spoon, sitting at their rickety table in grim silence until the very last drop was gone. Afterward, they lay down fully dressed on their bed with their curtain still open.

This episode haunted me for a long time. I could not forget our roommates' desperate haste. I felt at the same time guilty for having more food than they and ashamed for them, for their frenzy. It was my first conscious awareness of someone else's misery. Although food was constantly on my mind – no matter how much I was given, I always wanted more – I did not yet realize that we too were living on the edge of survival. It was only some two years later that I began to wonder how Mama managed to feed us every day. She was hoarding and rationing our supplies with such discipline, and always feeding me first, that food seemed to somehow multiply by itself; the miracle of manna from heaven was nothing compared to Mama's amazing achievements.

Papa was working as an administrator at the Kambarka district school and was paid about the same salary as

Volodya's mother. Every month he brought home enough money to purchase approximately one-half of one egg. 'If at least we could buy a whole, entire egg,' Mama joked, 'it would be less messy!'

In addition to his princely wages, Papa received a sporadic allowance of vodka. Much more than rubles, vodka was the real currency of the land. It could be swapped for almost anything, even access to the authorities. Nothing worked as well as a discreet offering of vodka when one needed a signature on a residency permit, a travel permit to a neighboring town, or any official paperwork. Logs for the stove, felt boots for winter, a warmly padded jacket, everything and anything could be conjured up with vodka. If only we had more of it!

While Papa's vodka allotment helped immeasurably, it was Mama who put food on the table with her skills at bartering, gathering, and tilling a small plot of land. Bartering usually took place at the Sunday morning bazaar, an open-air market where the local Udmurt, Russians, and Tatars mingled with the newcomers. Even the privileged *Neftebaza* wives, who had their own commissary, came shopping at the bazaar.

Mama was slowly bartering away the precious possessions remaining from the parcels that my grandmothers had sent to Kuma. These included several packets of sewing needles. Mama sold off the needles one at a time during the first winter, her fingers numb from the cold. A good sewing needle was so valuable that it could easily fetch several eggs or a small bag of kasha. At last, when the second winter came, Mama had nothing left except a hand-embroidered night-gown made of heavy, peach-colored silk, a keepsake from our prewar life. She did not want to part with it, it was her talisman, but in the end she sold it for a large sum of money to a *Neftebaza* woman who urgently needed a new ballgown for the all-important New Year's Eve party; Russian women were notorious for their predilection for Polish nightgowns, which they wore as formal attire.

With Mama's sale of her silk nightgown, several loaves of bread, melted butter, eggs, kasha and even a small tin of tea made their appearance. This bounty was added to the potatoes, carrots and onions that we had planted ourselves.

Mama and I grew the carrots and onions in the small communal garden where every tenant in our building was allowed the use of a tiny strip of dirt. The carrot seeds and the sections of onion ready for sprouting had been a gift from a Tatar peasant who was one of Mama's friends. She gave us the seeds sewn in a bit of cloth and the onions wrapped in a page from an old newspaper. We tilled the soil, then mixed it with droppings from the chickencoop in the courtyard and some human waste from the stinking heap behind the outhouse. We watered and we weeded, we endured incursions by scavengers and petty thieves, we didn't quite know what we were doing, but in the end we had several bucketfuls of carrots and onions.

We also had several bushels of potatoes that were supposed to last us till the next harvest, now that Mama's bartering days were coming to an end. Small, dark and lumpy, still matted with little clumps of dirt, our tubers in no way resembled the beautiful cylindrical spuds from today's supermarkets, but they were tasty and nutritious, and our bulwark against the winter.

We were very proud of our harvest, which we owed mostly to Mama's toil. But, in a perfect illustration of the system of *po blatu*, we owed our 'access' to the potato field to Papa's position at the district school. With so many teachers – most of the young men and many of the women – away at the front, the smaller schools from the surrounding villages were closed and the entire school system was consolidated into a single district school. The principal was an important person in town, and Papa, who was taking care of bookkeeping and all of the day-to-day administration, was important to the principal. Hence our 'access' to a small section of a potato field that ostensibly belonged to the local *kholkhoz* [collective farm].

When it came time to plant in the first spring, Mama still had a few things left to barter. She swapped a wool scarf for a supply of potatoes that were studded with eyes. She told me that by cutting a potato into sections with one eye apiece we would sprout a whole new potato from each eye. It was amazing. My parents began by pushing a cartload of dried excrement from behind the outhouse all the way to our potato field. I had to go with them because they wouldn't let me stay in the house alone. It was incredibly far, almost 5 km from our house. The field was infamous for its location 'by the 5th kilometer'. They worked the dried excrement carefully into the ground by turning the earth over and over again with a spade. They planted neat rows of potato sections, placing each one carefully, with its eye pointing down. They fetched pail after pail of water from a nearby well and trickled the water down between each row. When at last they were done, I was exhausted from watching them and from running around. That field was probably very small, perhaps smaller than a room, but to my five-year-old brain it loomed very large and I was incredibly proud of my parents' achievement. We all scrubbed our hands carefully with the scratchy earth and rinsed them several times before trudging back. When I complained of being tired, Papa hoisted me on his shoulders and carried me all the way home. I was ten feet tall. It was one of the happiest days in my life.

Mama often worked in our field, weeding and watering it. I loved pulling out weeds around the delicate, white potato flowers while Mama went to fetch the heavy pails of water from the *kholkhoz* well. The potatoes were constantly thirsty. Our summers in Kambarka were as hot as our winters were cold, and the earth was parched. A merciless sun hung immobile in the sky, just ahead of me and to my right. One morning, I had a brilliant idea: why not catch up with the sun by running as fast as I could until I would find myself just below its orb? I ran and ran till my lungs were about to burst open, and still the sun was exactly where it had been before, hanging just ahead of me and to my right. I ran again, and again the sun stayed ahead of me.

'Why can't I catch up with the sun, Mama?' I asked.

'Why do you always have to ask stupid questions?' she snapped. It was so unfair! The inquisitive child of two people who were both reluctant to part with information, and too young to grasp this vast mismatch between our temperaments, I was driving my parents to distraction with my incessant 'Whys?' and 'How come?'

On our way home, we sometimes stopped to greet acquaintances from the village. Most were either Udmurt or

Russian, though to me they all looked the same, as many of the Udmurt had reddish-blond hair, notwithstanding their Mongol origins. But even I could tell the Tatars from afar, especially the women, with their colorful kerchiefs and their kaftans that were fitted at the waist over long, heavy skirts. They walked with a light step and radiated a certain air of freedom. On several occasions, I even saw Tatar women urinating standing up in the street, completely at ease under the shelter of their skirts. Mama looked disgusted, muttering, 'Just like a cow' under her breath, but I thought it was fascinating.

Mama had a Tatar friend, a widow who lived by herself in a small *izba* by the edge of the village and who, for some unfathomable reason, actually owned a cow. We had first met her when we went to her hut to buy a glass of milk for me and we continued to visit whenever Mama had a bit of money. The milk was often still fresh from the cow, still warm and foamy, and faintly redolent of the stable. The two women chatted while I was drinking. The Tatar woman spoke of her four children, two daughters and two sons who were fighting the fascist invaders, and Mama talked about our family who were under the fascist boot. Oddly enough, though they both spoke broken Russian, they seemed to draw comfort from each other.

In the end, we fared much better than this generous Tatar woman, as some of our relatives survived while she lost all four of her children. I wish I could remember her name, for she was a warm-hearted, giving woman who always greeted us with a kind word and a smile. Her body shriveled and the light seeped out of her eyes as her children were killed one by one: the sons on the battlefield and the daughters bearing stretchers with the wounded at the front lines. I still think of this nameless Tatar woman whenever anyone mentions the 20 million dead of the Great Patriotic War.

Almost every Soviet family had someone who was 'away at the Front'. The oldest son of our upstairs neighbors had just been drafted. We saw him leave wearing his best *rubacha* [Russian shirt] and his only pair of boots, and carrying the rest of his belongings in a bundle on his back.

How I wished it were his younger brother, Volodya, leaving

instead! Volodya from upstairs was about the same age as Volodya our roommate but, while the latter was completely harmless, the former was truly evil. His skull was shaved to keep away the lice. He was short and stocky, with a malicious gleam in his eyes. He gave me the shivers. One summer day, Volodya cornered me by the shed in the courtyard and informed me, 'in complete confidence and for my own protection', that a family of small, black devils were living in our room, so well hidden that no one had ever been able to find them. They roamed only at night and they never revealed themselves to an adult. They were interested only in little children. They would wait until a little girl was asleep before swooping down to lacerate her face and her eyes with their razor-sharp claws. That same afternoon, Volodya followed up his 'warning' with a pantomime act. He came peeking into our window and pretended to lacerate his own face with his long, filthy fingernails.

Everyone knew that devils, demons and goblins were lurking everywhere, so I naturally believed every word of Volodya's tale. I was terrified. The little devils, with their bloodstained claws and their leering faces that looked just like Volodya's, materialized as soon as my eyes would close. It was as if my eyelids were forming the backdrop for the apparition. There was nothing I could do to stave them off but resist sleep with all my might. My stuffed rabbit, Pufciu Cylinder, helped a little bit, but not much. At last, after several nights full of torment, I succeeded in outwitting the little devils simply by burrowing ostrich-like under my pillow. But my victory was shallow, as I remained addicted to the protection of that pillow for as long as we lived in Kambarka. Even after we moved to our own one-room *izba*, Volodya's devils were always hovering at a mere pillow's distance away from me.

My parents sensed that something was wrong. Mama even told Papa, 'I don't know what is wrong with the child, she is not sleeping and she is losing weight.' Yet, true to my life-long practice of keeping my troubles to myself, I never told my parents about Volodya and the devils. I don't know why, I just didn't. Perhaps I sensed that they had enough troubles of their own, perhaps I was afraid of their scoffing, as Papa was especially quick to ridicule me. It may be that I already understood the limits of their power, or maybe it is simply the way of introverted children.

For all the restlessness of my nights, daytime was always fresh and exciting. One day, for example, Mama came home with a small chick that she named Pepitko because his plumage reminded her of a coat she had once owned, made of a black-and-white fabric with a twilled weave called *pepito*. The plan was to fatten up Pepitko until he grew big enough to be eaten. We were feeding him bits of bread and some grain that Mama brought from I don't know where, and he was also digging all over the courtyard for worms and tiny pebbles. Pepitko would come to snatch a tiny piece of bread or a single grain clenched between Mama's teeth; he even tried to peck at her teeth when there was nothing there. Mama looked so young and beautiful, with her dazzling white teeth and her copper-brown hair gleaming in the sun! We laughed so hard that the neighbors came out to watch the spectacle.

But when the time came to slaughter Pepitko, Mama could not bring herself to wring his neck and, because we could not afford to let him grow into a rooster, she bartered him away at the Sunday morning bazaar. Although I had forgotten even the taste of meat, I was glad nonetheless, as I would have been unable to swallow Pepitko's flesh. Within our hearts we were still squeamish city-dwellers, always ready to eat meat as long as someone else had done the slaughtering, with none of the local villagers' honest pragmatism.

Summer evenings lasted a long time at our northern latitude. Children dawdled in the street, old people sat outdoors on narrow wooden chairs, men and women were going about their chores, chopping wood and fetching water from the communal well, some 500 meters away from our house. One balmy late summer evening, as Papa and I were on our way to the well, we met a small group of recently released Polish ex-deportees like ourselves. The adults, as ever, were talking about the war, this time about a huge new battle brewing around a distant city called Stalingrad. It seemed to me that they were all dejected by the news from the front, though no one would have dared to acknowledge it openly, but I was only half-listening. I was too busy playing with my friend Witek Nowacki.

When I had met Witek for the first time, I could not help staring at him. His dark brown hair was thickly streaked with greyish-white strands, as if someone had splashed him with dirty white paint. The amazing thing was that he had turned grey overnight during the bombardment of Warsaw in September of 1939, when he remained trapped for 24 hours under the rubble of his house, with the dead body of his father next to him. Despite his disconcerting appearance, which from a distance made him look like an aging dwarf, Witek was an irrepressible eight-year-old boy. His enthusiasm for life was contagious – a welcome antidote to the apathy of our roommate Volodya. I was so enthralled by Witek, so flattered by his attention to a girl not yet six, that I began to show off like a fool. While the adults were chatting, we were jumping down from a boulder that was much too high for me. Everything went well for the first two or three leaps but then I missed my footing and my left ankle gave way with a cracking sound when I landed. A blinding pain exploded into a thousand shooting stars. Papa carried me home and I was put to bed.

Our friend Dr Fishkin stopped by the following morning to palpate my badly sprained ankle, which was all tinged with purple. In his clipped surgeon's voice he told me to get out of bed and try to walk a little.

'No! No! I can't walk, it hurts too much! No!' I shrieked, turning to Mama for moral support.

'Do as Dr Fishkin tells you,' she replied, her voice radiating disapproval. There was nothing I could do. They were all ganging up against me. I gingerly placed my bare ankle on the bare floor and hobbled about until a wave of nausea washed all over me. They put me back to bed. I lay there facing the wall, sobbing from disillusion as much as pain: my Mama could be mean and stupid, and she always sided with other grown-ups.

Oddly enough, I was not angry with Dr Fishkin; on the contrary, I was feeling sorry for this tormented man whose wife held him responsible for the death of their daughter Lyuba. I was well aware of this tragic story because Mrs

Fishkin, herself a physician, kept telling and retelling it to anyone who would listen – even a little girl such as I. It was very unsettling to listen to, as it made me feel that there were two different women living in a single body; one whose mind had gone unhinged, and the other who functioned quite well as a caring mother to her surviving son Lonya, and who was a competent pediatrician at the Kambarka dispensary.

The Fishkins were evacuees from Minsk, a city that had fallen to the Germans shortly after the June 1941 invasion. During the panic and chaos which preceded the occupation of the city, Mr Fishkin was in charge of transporting the sick and wounded from his hospital to an evacuation train. He had in his pocket a precious piece of paper, a permit to evacuate Mrs Fishkin and the two children in that same hospital-train. Other doctors who had such permits first made sure to place their families on the train, before running back for their patients. Mr Fishkin, putting his loyalty to his patients above his duty to his family, did things in reverse order. Lyuba was killed by a German bomb just before he finally showed up to fetch them.

Mrs Fishkin never forgave her husband for Lyuba's death. Under normal circumstances she might have kicked him out or left him, but where was one to go when there was no housing? And so they stayed together in the dank semi-basement room where they lived with little Lonya, who spent a great deal of time sitting on a frayed velveteen sofa that was the color of vomit. I can still see myself standing behind that disgusting sofa while Mrs Fishkin injected me and the pasty-faced Lonya with a vaccine which was supposed to protect us from a dreadful disease called diphtheria–tetanus–typhus. With her left hand, she grabbed the skin at the base of my neck, just above my left shoulder blade, and with her right she stabbed me with an enormous needle. The vaccine made me ill with a very high fever for several days.

At some point during the summer of 1943, we were granted permission to move to a one-room *izba* that we would not be required to share with anyone. The blessings of privacy were to be ours at long last! I did not know that someone had interceded on our behalf with the housing authorities, nor did

I care. Of course, like everyone else, big and small, I guessed that things were seldom as they appeared, but I would have never thought to question the mysterious workings of the *po blatu* system, had that system itself not demanded an offering from me. Mama took my precious stuffed rabbit, my beloved Pufciu Cylinder – the only thing that was truly mine since the loss of my doll Falunia – and gave him to a *Neftebaza* child. 'Beloved child,' she said to me by way of explanation, 'there is someone at the *Neftebaza* to whom we owe a great debt of gratitude.'

We never mentioned Pufciu again. I could not bring myself to talk about him – I was choking up at the mere thought of him – and Mama, to her credit, understood that apologies would serve only to worsen my heartbreak. My small world was shattered. Even today, almost 60 years later, I still feel a pang of loss and betrayal when I think of Pufciu Cylinder's sacrifice to the common good.

6 151 Karl Marx Street

Our *izba* was located at 151 Karl Marx Street. A broad, long thoroughfare, Karl Marx was Kambarka's main street, yet there was no need to worry about traffic as in all my years there I saw fewer than half a dozen trucks and not a single car. During the summer season, the wind blew clouds of dust and tufts of animal hair studded with burrs. Everything turned to mud during the *rasputitsa*, the rainy season, while in winter snowdrifts often piled as tall as our house.

The *izba* had two double-glazed windows which faced the street. The entrance door was to the side, beyond a low picket fence and a patch of dirt. A small, windowless vestibule served as a storage area and a buffer zone against the winter cold. The room itself was dwarfed by a mammoth *Ruskaya pieczka* (Russian stove), the traditional combination of wood-burning stove and sleeping loft that is the nerve center of any *izba*. One couldn't see either the stove-pipe or the flue, as both were cleverly built into a thick partition fashioned of baked clay. On the other side of this partition, a warm sleeping loft was resting on top of a baked clay platform that extended all the way to the back wall. The stove and the platform were like siamese twins joined at the back by the heated partition.

Though the locals snuggled up on their lofts during the long winter nights, we never slept on ours. I was even forbidden to play there because bedbugs and other pests loved to nest in little crevices behind the stove. While most of our neighbors seemed resigned to living with bedbugs, fleas, head-lice and crab-lice, Mama was waging a never-ending war against vermin. Her weapons of choice were blowing smoke in all the cracks and dabbing them with kerosene from our lamp. One day, she almost set fire to the house. But, thanks to her maniacal determination, we remained more or less free of infestation – a state of affairs that in my blissful ignorance I took completely for granted.

My parents' bed stood in the back corner next to the sleeping loft. I slept at the foot of their bed in an ancient crib that was surrounded by a string net. The crib was much too short for me and I was forced to curl up along its diagonal. One morning I woke up with my head wedged inside the net in an agonizingly painful twist, and the most horrible crick in my neck. I was panicstricken. Mama quickly ran to fetch her friend Diedushko (little grandfather), a skillful bone-setter who was renowned for his 'golden hands'. I myself had observed Diedushko calming down an ailing horse and I trusted him more than I trusted Dr Fishkin – and so, it seemed, did Mama.

Diedushko placed his gnarled hands on the back of my neck and began talking to me soothingly, as if I were a horse. 'Don't you worry *dievotchka* [little girl],' he said, 'we'll have you straightened out in no time.' Just as I was beginning to relax a little bit, Diedushko rudely grabbed my neck in the vise of his hands and untwisted it in one swift movement. We all heard it snapping back into position. He told Mama to keep me comfortable with a warm towel on the back of my neck and then left abruptly, without giving her a chance to feel ashamed of having not a thing to offer him to drink: no tea, no vodka, only water from the well.

While the local people tended to be short and stocky, Diedushko was tall and lanky. A widower who lived alone in an *izba* similar to ours, he had once been a *kulak* in the Ukraine, one of those relatively wealthy peasants whom Stalin had singled out for punishment during his savage campaign of collectivization. Countless thousands were put to death, while the more fortunate among them, such as Diedushko, were dispossessed and sent into exile. Needless to say, I was told nothing about Diedushko's past. I knew only that he had come from the Ukraine many years before the war and that he was not an evacuee like the other Ukrainians in town.

Diedushko and I didn't speak very much, but I sensed that he too was an 'other' and I felt safe watching him work in his little yard. Using only his axe with a birchwood handle – which he deemed the only type of handle worth having so long as the wood has been properly dried in a *bania* [communal sauna] – he was building next to his vestibule a lean-to as snug as an *izba*. It is from Diedushko that I learned how a proper *izba* should be built without a single nail, merely through a skillful molding of the logs. He used his axe to carve out in one log a groove in which its companion log would fit in a completely weathertight way. He could effortlessly split wood into thin, flat sections or into elegant, delicate *ciurki* [kindling wood] – so different to the misshapen, tortured little wedges that Papa painstakingly hacked out for us.

I was now sleeping with my parents until a new bed could be found for me. Mama bartered away my old cot for some badly needed food – we were going through a very lean period – then she set out in search of a new straw mattress. We ended up at the house of a crusty old lady called Utka, who did a lot of sewing and patching. Her little *izba* was dazzlingly clean. The wide floorboards were scrubbed to a buttery yellow with handfuls of sand, the lace curtains were snow-white, a big samovar stood gleaming in a corner and several wooden ladles, painted in bright red and gold, hung on the wall next to the stove. I had never seen anything so beautiful, but it was all as nothing, compared to Utka's wonderful carved bed that was festooned with a gorgeous skirt of white lace peeking from below a thick, rich scarlet quilt. Like many among the older peasants, Utka rarely slept in her bed, which was used only on special occasions. Amid the drabness of everyday life, the real purpose of Utka's bed was to be a thing of beauty in and of itself.

Utka had a great many different needles of all sizes and many scraps of fabric recycled from old clothing and old bedding. She stuffed some ticking recovered from an old featherbed with soft, clean straw and made me a very comfortable mattress. I was so thrilled with it that I wanted to sleep on it right away, but both my parents threw a fit of hysterics.

'*Erbarm doch, erbarm doch! Wos wilst du frum mi'e huben?*' [Have pity on me, have pity on me! What do you want from me?] Papa moaned.

'It does not even bear talking about! My child is not going to sleep on the floor, like some slave in Egypt!' Mama screeched.

Even though we had all slept on the floor many times before, something about the prospect of my sleeping there in our new *izba* had touched a very raw nerve in both of them. Fortunately, the crisis was defused after Mama and Diedushko used some old planks to make a nice platform for my new mattress. My new bed was placed by the window in the corner located to the right of the entrance, opposite the stove. The table and chairs that had initially stood there were moved to the opposite corner, by the window facing my parents' bed.

Thanks to our *izba*'s southern exposure, our two windows gave us ample light during the day. We had no electricity for the evening but we did have a radio of sorts. A large megaphone with a broad, scalloped rim like in the old-fashioned Victrolas, it flared out from a dark box attached to the wall between the two windows, just below the ceiling. I called it the 'giant ear'. It was connected to a radio located somewhere in town, and every evening it brought the 10 p.m. news broadcast from Moscow into our house. I don't recall any of us ever using the on/off switch on the 'giant ear'. I certainly didn't, but that was because children in my parents' world were forbidden to touch anything that had switches, dials or knobs. There was no need for my parents to bother with switches, as that mysterious radio somewhere in the village was apparently brought to life by an invisible hand only for the duration of the daily news from the Front. No matter how fast asleep, I always woke up on my own a few seconds before 10 p.m. and I was sitting upright in my bed when the powerful, riveting voice of newscaster Levitan began to boom.

'*Vnimanye, vnimanye, govorit Moskva! Slushaytie nashe radioperedatchi!*' [Attention, attention, this is Radio Moscow speaking! Listen to our broadcasts!]

A dramatic pause would follow. Then, after a hypnotizing '*Sevodnia . . .*' [Today. . .], followed by the recitation of the date, Levitan would read the latest official bulletin from the Front.

He would invoke eternal glory for those who fell in heroic defense of the Motherland, and he would call for death to the German invaders. The communiqué was signed by Stalin, Supreme Commander and Marshal of the Soviet Union.

We all listened in absolute silence to Levitan's incantatory voice. Mama and Papa were thinking about their parents, their friends and all of our relatives. Months became years and still we had no news of our loved ones. O how we prayed for their survival! How we longed to go home again!

Titanic battles were raging along thousands of kilometers. Millions of Soviet dead were paving our way home, yet the enemy was like many-headed Hydra: no sooner was one of its heads severed than another would grow in its place.

Mama was making me pray every evening to Dziadziusio Schreiber. I was asking him to protect our family in Poland, to shield us all from harm, to crush Hitler and to bring us safely home to Kraków. There was never any reference to God in these prayers, perhaps because religious worship was frowned upon by the authorities, or simply because Mama had an anthropomorphic view of God and confused Him with Dziadziusio Schreiber. She had never recovered from her father's death in 1935, and often talked aloud to him as if he were in the room, something that unsettled me greatly. (Talking to a dead grandfather in one's prayers at night was one thing, but talking to him in broad daylight was another!)

Our house was becoming a gathering place for our friends, most of whom still lived in communal arrangements – four or five to a room, or worse. Mama had made a kind of privacy curtain around my bed, from an old homespun sheet that was almost velvety after countless washings. It was comforting to fall asleep to the soothing murmur of conversation and the dance of shadows flickering behind my curtain in the dim light of the kerosene lamp.

Every so often, Mama and Papa would both go out together at night. As a rule, it was Papa who attended meetings, but Mama went with him to compulsory gatherings and other exercises in political education. On such evenings, Tamara Nun, the daughter of neighbors who lived across the street, would come to watch over me. She was a soft-spoken, slim redhead with thick, shiny braids, who always wore the red scarf of a Pioneer under the collar of her blouse. As I was allowed to stay up late on those occasions, I would read while Tamara did her homework. This was a great treat for me. Ordinarily, I was forbidden to read in the evening, since Mama always kept the light very dim in order to conserve fuel. All my protestations, all my assurances that I could see well enough to read even though the light was dim, fell on deaf ears. 'That's all we need now, for you to ruin your eyes with all this reading in the dark,' was Mama's response. However, when Tamara was there, Mama would crank up the knob on the kerosene lamp until a warm, soft light appeared instead of the usual smoky sputtering.

If she hadn't been a redhead like her father, it would have been difficult to imagine that Tamara was her parents' daughter, or even her brother's sister. The three of them were as coarse as she was sensitive. It's not that I disliked her baby brother Tolya, who was about my age. To the contrary, I liked him a lot. He was a tubby, cheerful little fellow who would come bouncing into our house like a noisy ball, always ready to play. The Nuns lived across the street, about two or three houses to our left, in a house that had two bedrooms and a living room. Mr Nun was a *shyshka* [big wheel] at the *Neftebaza*. I don't know what he did there, but his job must have provided him with access to great quantities of food. He and his wife were the only overweight people I ever saw in Kambarka: she had a triple chin cascading down to her ample bosom, and he could never quite manage to button his shirt over his enormous belly. He often came strolling into our little yard after supper. He would stand there rubbing his gut with a sigh of satisfaction and exclaim '*Plotno pokushali*'. It is impossible to do justice in English to this little Russian phrase, which literally means 'We ate heartily.' Perhaps a Frenchman describing a delicious meal with an affectionate '*On a bien mangé!*' [did we have a good meal!] would understand the full impact of Mr Nun's '*Plotno pokushali.*'

Mr Nun was so naive in his insensitivity that I could not be really angry at him. He truly did not realize that everyone around him was going to bed hungry. It was Mrs Nun that I detested for her crass hypocrisy in pretending that there was no food in their house. Mama knew that Mrs Nun would not give me any snack when I was playing there, so she always gave me a slice of bread to take with me. But Tolya would prance into our house empty-handed, even at snack time. His cheery *'Tiotia Ania, ya opiat' chleboushka zabyl'* [Auntie Ania, I again forgot to bring my little piece of bread] still rings in my ears. Mama would give him a slice of bread – more often than not her own portion for supper. 'I already ate,' she would say later while handing Papa and me our slices.

The Nuns, who had more food than any of our acquaintances, were breaking an unspoken rule of Kambarka etiquette which stipulated that children should bring their own snacks to avoid embarrassing their hosts, whose cupboard may have been bare. A similar rule applied to grown-ups, who either brought some scrap as an offering or claimed that they had 'just finished eating' and were totally stuffed. Mama was not easily fooled by false assurances of having 'just eaten' and I saw her several times slipping a piece of bread to people like our friend Malwina, a young woman from Warsaw who had even less than we did.

It was a time when we still had real bread – a dark peasant rye that Mama cut into very thin slices. After toasting my slice on top of the stove, I sometimes rubbed it on one side with a bit of garlic. No bread that I have eaten since – and I have had my fair share of the most delicious – has ever come close to tasting as good as that slice of garlic-flavored rye. I also had a passion for buckwheat kasha, which Mama used to bring from the bazaar in the days when she still had something to barter. As 1944 approached, however, the taste of kasha became a memory. As long as the weather remained warm, we managed with our little crops and foraging for ferns or weeds such as dandelions and nettles. Thickened with a bit of flour, nettles made tasty soups. We picked a great many of them once we learned how to avoid touching the stinging surface hairs which made our skin erupt with itchy, oozing blisters. After the cold weather set in, Mama learned the proper way to cook the bitter *kalina* berries, to make them edible. Kalina (guelder rose) trees had small clusters of beautiful, bright orange berries that remained on the tree over the winter and the villagers showed Mama how to make them into a filling for a kind of tart they prepared from a dough of flour and water.

That winter was especially bitter, the more so after a part of our potato crop froze because we had not mastered the proper techniques of storage. Frozen raw potatoes – and I am not talking about French fries from a supermarket freezer, which are preprocessed and precooked – genuinely raw frozen potatoes are utterly disgusting, and their stench unbelievably sickening. Hungry though we were, we had to throw out a good part of our potato crop from the 'fifth kilometer'.

I developed boils all over my body from malnutrition. The worst was a huge, extremely painful abcess on my back that would not heal for months. Nevertheless, my seventh birthday, which we celebrated in the midst of all this gloom, was a joyful occasion. Mama had a present for me. She had conjured up from somewhere a small piece of something sweet that had dark whorls of sugar paste flavored with cocoa and whitish whorls made of a plain sugar paste. The ultimate delicacy, however, was an orange that our friend, Mr Parnes, brought me as a present from a *komandirovka* [business trip] to the provincial capital of Izhevsk.

Mr Parnes, a sweet man with big, wistful eyes, was constantly talking about his wife and child, who were trapped under the Germans in Poland. Saying that I reminded him of his little girl, he would sometimes stop by to bring me a book, some scraps of paper or anything useful that he could find. On the afternoon of my birthday, Mr Parnes, with a great display of theatrics and a triumphant twinkle in his eye, extracted from his pocket an orange wrapped in a clean white handkerchief. I just sat there like a dummy, looking at this amazing object, but fortunately Mama, ordinarily a most understated person, quickly picked up the festive mood and, pretending to be a magician, transformed my orange into a bright 'flower'. With her knife, she scored the skin of the orange into eight identical sections, cutting through to the flesh. With her fingers, she peeled back each section of skin, leaving it attached at the base, and folded it inward to form a crown around the fruit. Then she gently pulled apart the sections of the flesh itself to complete my 'flower', which she handed to me with much ceremony.

Shortly after my birthday, we woke up one morning to complete darkness. There was an eerie stillness in the house. Everything, the roof, the windows, the door, was buried under snowdrifts. When we tried to push the door open, it yielded only a crack that quickly filled with snow. Mama wanted to poke a broom handle through this crack but the opening was too small. We pushed the door again and again until it gave another crack which in turn filled with snow. This time, Mama was able to poke her broom about and loosen up a bit more snow which, luckily for us, was very fluffy. My parents worked for a long time, scooping handfuls of snow into the vestibule. We melted them on top of the stove, where huge masses of powdery white were reduced to a mere pailful. When at last the front door was fully opened and a narrow canyon dug all the way to the gate in the picket fence, we felt much safer. It took many hours to clear the windows, the woodshed, and a path to the outhouse. We kept melting snow for drinking and cooking until the road to the well became passable again. Nobody plowed the street; instead, everyone cleared a passage from his house to the next, so that pedestrians could enjoy a continuous walkway while sleds had the middle of the street all to themselves.

The *Neftebaza*, with its small fleet of trucks, had its own clearing crew, but the vital job of clearing the train tracks in the area fell to the citizenry, most especially the older schoolchildren, those old enough to be Komsomols, who were called upon after every storm. It was a patriotic duty that no one was allowed to shirk. Even Papa and other able-bodied workers were sometimes recruited to help keep the railway lines open.

Winter was beautiful despite its brutality. Frost patterns shimmered on the window pane like a kaleidoscope; fat icicles were glinting in the sun below the roof; packed snow made dry, crunchy noises under my boots and powdery snow was great for sinking into like a corpse; fir trees sparkled merrily and soft, silvery birches projected long, skinny shadows onto the dazzling white. Yet the cold was so intense that Mama was constantly checking me for signs of frostbite, especially after Papa's earlobes became frostbitten, even though he always wore the flaps of his *shapka* hat pulled down over his ears.

Poor Papa was forced to trudge about wearing *lapcies* – a kind of footwear woven from flexible birch bark and stuffed with rags and newspapers for warmth – as we could never find any *valenki* [warm boots made of thick felt] large enough to fit him. He was also so much taller than the average Russian that the sleeves of his brown *fufaika* [winter jacket padded with cotton] were much too short for him.

Papa was in charge of most of the outdoor chores, such as fetching water from the communal well, chopping wood or keeping the outhouse from overflowing. This meant that every so often he had to chop up the frozen mass of excrement and to dispose of it behind the outhouse. As there was very little room there, my fiercely scrupulous father once stooped to a bit of clandestine disposal. He threw some frozen excrement over the fence onto our next-door-neighbors' pile. They were a swarming household with eight children and two grandparents, and Papa was convinced that nobody would notice a bit of extra waste, but he was wrong.

Our irate neighbor came by to threaten us with immediate retaliation in kind should we ever again attempt to throw our waste over the fence.

'*U nas bolshe. My was zakidayem!*' [We have more of it. We'll outthrow you all right! We'll bury you! You'll never catch up with us] he yelled.

Papa, who always made a tragedy of everything, was very upset but Mama broke into a fit of frenzied laughter as soon as our neighbor left. She laughed so hard that she could not even speak. 'I bet you that none of them is the least bit constipated,' she finally managed to stammer.

One day, when Papa came home from work, Mama noticed a little piece of paper pinned inside his *fufaika*. It was a note consisting of two words – '*Ya revnuyu*' [I am jealous] – followed by the name of one of the teachers. Short though it was, this little note caused a major row in the house. Mama was so furious that she forgot that I was there.

'I knew it, I knew it! They all want to get inside your pants!' she shrieked. Why was this teacher jealous of Papa, she demanded to be told, and who was she jealous of? Papa swore that he did not know anything about it.

'I have it up to here with all those hysterical women! Do you really think that I would be stupid enough to leave such a note in my coat if I had anything to do with this?' he shouted.

They calmed down eventually and never fought in my presence again but the air hung heavy in our house for some time. The problem, of course, was due to the loneliness of the women teachers whose husbands were mostly away at the Front. They swarmed around Papa and vied for his attention. I observed the spectacle myself after I started school later that year.

Though women were always attracted to Papa, I truly think, even now with the benefit of hindsight, that he loved Mama and was faithful to her. Besides, he was much too prudent to get involved in a potentially explosive situation. It was so easy to end up in a gulag should a jealous mistress whisper a few words to the NKVD about an alleged anti-Soviet statement.

Grown-ups kept disappearing without warning. I well remember what happened to poor Mr Parnes about a year later, after Poland was already liberated and news about the full extent of the Shoah began to trickle in. When he learned that his wife and daughter were dead, Mr Parnes became so despondent that he no longer cared about anything, not even himself. One morning, he flatly refused to go and help clear the railway tracks after a snowstorm. 'Hitler killed my wife and my child and now Stalin wants to kill me as well,' he complained. Mr Parnes was taken away and we never saw him again.

We also knew a Mr Tauber, a Polish Jew who spoke only Yiddish and a bit of mangled Russian mixed with 'Polyiddish'. I remember him well because he had a very oily face with a bulbous nose that was studded with monstrous blackheads. I thought him repulsive. Poor Mr Tauber had a sick wife with a badly abscessed arm that needed a change of dressing several times a day. Showing up late for work one morning, he tried to explain his situation to his supervisor. '*Mojej zinki ruczka bolit,*' he said to the man, in a hilarious mixture of Polish, Yiddish, and Russian, while vigorously slapping his own arm. There is no point in attempting a translation, except to say that the supervisor, hearing something like 'my little wife's little arm is hurting,' sent Mr Tauber to jail for six months for the double offense of being late for work and pulling his superior's leg.

I remember several other people who disappeared overnight. My queries about them were explained away by their 'traveling on a *komandirovka*' [officially sanctioned business trip]. Needless to say, my parents were afraid of me and of what I might inadvertently reveal to the outside world. Luckily, owing mostly to my Victorian upbringing as a child who was supposed to be seen but not heard, I learned at a very early age to keep my mouth shut in the presence of others.

When we were alone at home, however, it was another matter. One memorable evening I demanded to be told why our Soviet friends, like the Fishkins and the Ginzburgs, were called 'evacuees', whereas we, the Poles, were called '*biezhency*', a word which in Russian means literally 'those who have run away'.

'If we have run away,' I said indignantly, 'then so have they. We all ran away from the fascist invaders.'

More than an issue of semantics, what bothered me was an uneasy feeling that somehow we were at the very bottom of the totem-pole, less worthy and less secure than the others. What bothered my parents, on the other hand, was my loose tongue – I was charging Soviet citizens who had been duly and officially evacuated by the authorities with the crime of 'running away' – and they hit the roof in their panic.

'This child is going to bring me to my grave,' moaned Mama.

'*Oi, vei's mir! Wos wilst du frum mi'e huben?*' groaned Papa. This was all too much for him. 'What did I ever do to deserve such a *hojkier* [a hunchback, a burden], such a *krime jukiel* [twisted nothing]? When will you ever stop asking questions like Nusen Figatner?', he yelled. (Poor Nusen Figatner was a mythical village idiot from Mielec who was renowned for his stupid questions, and I was often reminded of his existence.)

As if it were not enough to be a *hojkier* and a *krime jukiel*, I was also being picked on by the neighborhood kids, including the clan who lived next door. Now that summer was back, they were all running around barefoot in the dust and having a wonderful time. Mama did not allow me to play with them because they were ridden with lice. But in any case, I doubt that they would have been willing to accept me, since I was much more entertaining as an object of derision than as a playmate.

My garments were so bizarre that I might as well have been an alien from another planet. I had outgrown all of my normal clothes and Mama forced me to wear the only thing that still fitted: a pair of pink cotton pajamas with white trimming. Merry bands of kids were jeering and hooting whenever I appeared in that accursed costume. Things got even worse after Mama fashioned for me the most ridiculous shoes of two colors. She made them by attaching felt toe-pieces to an outgrown pair from which she had first painstakingly cut off the tips. I couldn't walk without waddling or run without tripping and still Mama refused to let me wear *lapcies*. As for going barefoot, it would have been absolutely unthinkable. 'My child shall have shoes even if it means that I have to stand upside down on my head,' she proclaimed. It was as if her self-respect and her essential being were mysteriously wrapped-up in my wearing what she called 'normal shoes'.

One day, as the jeering and hooting were getting out of hand, I ran to hide behind Mama's skirts while she was doing the laundry in our little yard.

Brandishing a bucket of scalding water that she had just brought out from inside the *izba*, Mama yelled at my tormentors in her broken Russian.

'You little ragamuffins, I'll pour *dill* all over you if you don't stop bothering my daughter!' She meant to say 'I'll pour *boiling water* all over you', but her Russian betrayed her. Unluckily for us, '*ukrop*', the Polish word for 'boiling water', means 'dill' in Russian.

The kids all laughed so hard they were holding onto their bellies. Poor Mama meant well but she too was helpless and I was worse off than before.

Yet Providence came to my rescue a few days later, as it always has at critical junctions of my life. I was again surrounded by a group of kids who were making fun of my attire but this time I stood my ground. In an uncontrollable impulse born of sheer desperation, I dropped the pants of those awful pink pajamas, and, yelling 'You can all kiss my ass for all I care!', I showed them all my naked behind.

I felt as if I were standing outside of myself, watching some other girl dropping her pants and mooning, but it worked. They left me alone afterward. They still persisted in calling me names like 'Oi, you!' or 'Little Jewess', but I did not really mind the name-calling, especially after Mama convinced me that I should be walking with my head high for being Jewish, that we belonged to a proud and ancient people who gave mankind its moral code of behavior. I did not really understand what she meant with all her big words but it was reassuring.

Overall, the brand of antisemitism that I personally experienced in Kambarka was relatively harmless. Nothing in it prepared me for my encounter with Polish Catholicism after our return to Kraków in 1946 – a confrontation so brutal and dehumanizing that it has left me scarred to this day. Even the shape of my nightmares was affected when Volodya's little black devils, by then reduced to a mildly unpleasant bedtime ritual, underwent a metamorphosis into the terrifying nightly vision of a vengeful Christ. His face still stained with black drops of blood from the crown of thorns, He was pointing a bony finger in my direction and mouthing hoarsely, 'Kill her, kill her, for she is a Christ-killer!'

However, back in the summer of 1944 in Kambarka, I was still deemed innocent of the crime of deicide. My main problem was a dearth of suitable playmates. As there were not any little girls within our circle of acquaintances, I spent a great deal of time by myself or with adults. Tolya Nun was still my friend, but he had his limitations and I could not stand his mother.

My favorite grown-ups were Masha and Alexander Ginzburg, whom I called 'Mamasha' and 'Papasha' [little mother and little father]. They and their two sons, Izi and Ruva, were refugees from Wilno (now Vilnius). Izi Ginzburg, who was about seventeen, was drafted, but miraculously he was not sent to the killing fields at the German front. He served his time in the Far East, where some troops were kept in readiness against a surprise Japanese attack. Ruva, the younger of the two boys, was about fourteen and still in school. Mamasha and Papasha were both dentists. They both had dark eyes and dark hair and they wore round glasses. Papasha had a round face, a merry twinkle in his eyes, and a talent for joke-telling. He taught me a bit of Yiddish and some hauntingly melodious Russian poems that I wish I could still remember. Papasha's rather homely face became almost handsome when he recited his beloved Lermontov or Pushkin, whose poetry he knew by heart.

Mamasha took care of my teeth. She taught me how to pull my baby teeth myself. I would wind one end of a string to the wobbly tooth and the other to the door knob, close the door and, presto, the tooth would pop out painlessly. Mamasha also filled some of my cavities, which she first inexplicably made bigger with an unsteady drill that she activated by moving a pedal up and down with her foot. Her enormous eyes would peer down from behind her thick lenses as she kept repeating 'Open wide! That's good. Come on! Open wide again!'

One day that summer I was invited to the *Neftebaza* compound to get acquainted with a new playmate – a little girl of my age. Mama went with me for tea in the afternoon in order to introduce me to the family. They sent a truck with a driver to pick us up, my very first ride since the beginning of the war. Like all the trucks I ever saw in Kambarka, it was fueled with wood chips through a furnace attached to the side of the cab. The furnace had a narrow chimney which spewed little puffs of black smoke when the motor was running. Mama and I climbed into the cab, next to the driver, and we took off. A swarm of children ran behind us in the dust, scrambling to climb onto the back of the truck.

The little girl and her mother greeted us very warmly and the mother called Mama 'Anna Abramovna'. The little girl took me to her room, where I played happily until the moment I saw my very own Pufciu Cylinder snuggled up with another stuffed animal. My heart skipped several beats, but the little girl did not even notice. She probably did not know that Pufciu was mine. Like a person in shock, I pretended to myself that I had not even seen my Pufciu, that he was not there.

Tea was served in a well-furnished room with shiny, polished floors and richly colored carpets. They gave me good bread with jam and butter but I could not swallow a single bite. A hard lump was constricting my throat and I had trouble breathing. I remember nothing else of that visit, yet I must have pulled myself together and managed to behave in a fairly normal fashion because they invited me again a few weeks later. I refused to go, and not even Mama was able to force me. I did not care if this caused her embarrassment or brought her trouble, I was not going to go to that house, and that was all there was to it.

Mama told the *Neftebaza* lady that I was not feeling well, an excuse that was actually true. There was indeed something wrong with me, my belly was aching, I was losing weight and had no energy. I was spending hours doodling listlessly on my slate, sitting at a miniature student desk that Papa had rescued from the school furnace. Even my books did not interest me.

Adding to the atmosphere of gloom in the house, our friend Malwina was lying very sick in my parents' bed. Mama nursed her for almost two weeks, feeding her from a little spoon and sponging her face with a damp towel. (Years later Mama told me that Malwina, an attractive young woman from Warsaw, had nearly died from a botched abortion.)

As for me, I was cured almost miraculously one morning after I went outside to relieve myself and passed an incredibly long tapeworm that had been the cause of my wasting away.

A few days before the beginning of the school year, Mama went to fetch water at the well and came back greatly distressed. Utka the seamstress had died after pricking herself with one of her needles. It seemed that the needle had somehow embedded itself completely inside her body, traveled to her heart and pierced it. The village was abuzz with excitement and speculation about this extraordinary occurrence. Everyone had a different explanation for it, yet the fact remained that Utka, of whom Mama and I were both very fond, was dead. The next day, Mama and I went to her house to pay our respects. I was not allowed to go inside the *izba* but managed to peek unobtrusively through the immaculate lace curtain. Utka, who used her magnificent bed only on very special occasions, was now lying there fully dressed, with her arms crossed on top of her chest. Two other old women were standing next to her and making the sign of the cross, a gesture that I had never seen before in the Soviet Union.

Without understanding why, I felt quite bereft after the loss of Utka. Like Diedushko, and one or two others who had come of age before the Revolution, they had a certain openness and an inner stillness that were somehow reassuring to me.

Like all Soviet children, I started school at the age of seven. As I could read and write fluently, while many of the children in my class had yet to learn their alphabet, the first-grade teacher did not know what to do with me. Eventually, I was transferred to a class where the pupils were all at least two years older than I. They were all paired neatly at desks built for two, except for one boy who sat by himself in the middle of the classroom. His name was Boris and he was to be my new deskmate. I slid onto the bench that was of one piece with the desk and sat there without moving for the remainder of the hour, with just here and there a quick glance in the direction of Boris. He was not so bashful. He looked me over with undisguised contempt: a girl, and a little one at that!

Under the watchful eye of my teacher, who wanted to please Papa, Boris was quiet and polite, but in reality we had an uneasy partnership that soon settled into a routine of mutual avoidance. Boris ignored me and I just tried to sit as far away from him as I could, trapped as we both were in the narrow space between our bench and our desk.

We had a sloping desktop that could be lifted to reveal a small compartment meant in principle for storing books and paper but empty in practice, as both books and paper were in very short supply. Most of the information was provided by the teacher, who spent a great deal of time writing on the blackboard. We were either writing on our slates or scribbling in the margins of old newspapers, which for some mysterious reason were always freely available.

Despite the shortages, despite my uneasy relation with Boris, I enjoyed school. My teacher was very good and, even when I was scribbling in the margins of old newspapers, there was something intrinsic to the process of learning that I found very satisfying. Little by little, I began to relax and even forgot about the hulking presence of Boris, who spent a great deal of time surreptitiously carving his initials into the scarred desktop.

Yet Boris must have been ever conscious of my presence. Perhaps he resented me for being different, for being small, and a foreigner; perhaps his classmates made fun of him for being stuck with me; perhaps he was simply bored. Be that as it may, one spring morning, swift as a lightning bolt, he suddenly sliced the inside of my left wrist with an open razor. He was so quick that I did not notice a thing until I saw all the blood. There was a lot of it. It was nothing serious, and I knew better than to tell tales to the teacher. I quickly wound my handkerchief around my wrist and covered the whole bloody mess with my sleeve, which also became soaked through. Back home, I told Mama that it was an accident, and she pretended to believe me. When I sat next to Boris the next morning, it was as if the air between us had been cleared. He no longer seemed to resent me and the rest of the school year passed uneventfully.

When Papa came home from work, I always ran to greet him as eagerly as if he had been gone for weeks. As soon as he appeared, I would jump on his feet and, grabbing hold of his waist, force him to walk me back and forth with my feet planted on top of his. My sun rose and set over my father, whom I idolized. Mama was the pillar of my life, but who pays much attention to a pillar when it is still standing?

My parents did not like open displays of affection and I was always starved for hugs and kisses. I was even more starved for compliments and expressions of approval, for both my parents were brought up to believe that complimenting a child was equivalent to spoiling her, and God forbid I should be spoiled in spite of – or rather precisely because of – our unstable circumstances.

Papa was already convinced that I was a dreamer who would be unable to cope later 'in life'. He called me 'Philosopher' and *Sędzia Sprawiedliwy* [a righteous judge] in a tone of voice that made me feel insignificant. In his mind he was still living in his *shtetl* and he expected me to think and feel exactly as he did, without any allowances for my own personality or the circumstances of our life in Kambarka. Neither he nor Mama had the slightest idea of what it meant to be a pupil in a class of older, rougher kids who tolerated me only because the teachers were watching out for my welfare.

Fortunately for me, I liked school itself and I accepted my isolation as something that could not be helped and wasn't even worth talking about, considering all our other problems. Besides, visions of food were now perpetually on my mind to the point that it was becoming difficult to concentrate in school or worry about my classmates.

The year 1944 was one of famine, especially after the cold weather set in. So many people were dying of starvation that the authorities began distributing something they called 'bread'. The loaves were made of a composite material in the shape of a brick where one could recognize bits of rotten potatoes and slivers of chopped up straw among other components of unknown origin. Mama was compulsive about inspecting every slice and crumbling it with her fingers before she would let me eat it because several people in the village had died of intestinal perforation after ingesting the sharp slivers of straw. This was not acknowledged officially, but Dr Fishkin, who had treated some of the emergencies, told us about it.

One afternoon, as I was reading a story about a girl who was eating kasha – it was in one of those little booklets that passed from hand to hand in an informal swapping library arrangement – my stomach began to growl. I could almost smell the delightful aroma of the kasha. Without thinking, I exclaimed, 'Oh, how I wish we could have some kasha!'

Mama did not say a word, though I could see that she was very upset. She left the room and began making busy noises in the dark vestibule. I could hear her pouring water from the pail into the tin-metal water dispenser that hung on the wall. We always kept that dispenser empty because it had a broken spigot, yet Mama did not seem to care that she was wasting precious water that had to be carried one pail at a time from a distant well. She continued banging objects in the vestibule for a while longer and then came back into the room as if nothing had happened.

A few days later, I noticed that her wedding ring was gone. This sent a shiver up my spine since I knew that Mama was saving this vestige of our bourgeois decadence for a dire emergency, for something ominous called '*czarna godzina*' [a dark hour]. However, my sense of foreboding evaporated as soon as I saw that she had brought some real bread and some eggs. She took three eggs and made an omelet for Papa and me in a small frying pan that we had not used for months. Setting the pan on the table between Papa and me while she herself remained standing by the stove, she told us, 'I already ate.'

Incredibly, in our excitement over the omelet, both Papa and I took this preposterous statement at face value. Running my knife exactly down the middle of the pan, I divided the omelet meticulously into two perfectly equal portions and solemnly warned Papa against crossing the 'border' between the two halves. 'Oh, what a *Sędzia Sprawiedliwy!*' exclaimed Papa in his disapproving tone of voice, and then he ruined my enjoyment of the feast completely by pretending to encroach on my half of the omelet. 'Stop crossing the border, Papa. It's not fair! It's not fair! Nothing is fair around here!' I whined.

With our nerves frayed by the endless waiting for news from our family in Poland, the three of us were becoming very jittery. Night after night we listened to announcer Levitan reading the Radio Moscow bulletin from the Front. After crossing into south-eastern Poland in mid-1944, the Red Army was moving west in fits and starts, and sometimes standing still for weeks or even months. At long last Kraków was liberated in January of 1945. Where was Grandmother Erna? And Grandmother Laura, and Grandfather Leib? And all the others? Was anyone still alive? Since the last postcard written in May of 1941, we had heard nothing from our loved ones.

As some among the community of Polish refugees began receiving news of their families through official organizations, the tragedy of the Shoah started to unfold for us. The Polish Jews were no more. There were almost no survivors. Our friends in Kambarka were walking like zombies, in shock, in grief, in rage and, above all, disbelief. No, it could not be, it was not possible that their loved ones were dead. Somehow, somewhere they would come out of hiding or be repatriated from a concentration camp. It just could not be.

As for us, it seems to me that we waited longer than most for news of our family. January of 1945 turned into February, then March, then April, and still we knew nothing. Mama, who had always been slim, now became emaciated, with deep, dark hollows under her eyes. She often talked to herself, mumbling some incomprehensible things about Hitler and his minions. And, to make matters worse, we were constantly hungry.

Providence came to our rescue in late winter or early spring of 1945. It must have been in late March, or perhaps early April, as the days were already growing longer but there was still snow on the ground. We received notification to pick up five packages addressed to us from abroad. This was quite unbelievable, as we never received any mail, much less packages, and even less from abroad. Mama and I brought the parcels home on Tolya Nun's sled, which we had borrowed for the occasion. We were pulling the sled and walking as fast as we could, since Mama did not want anyone to see us with our bounty, but, needless to say, we met an acquaintance and had no choice but to stop and chat with her. She happened to be very nosy and soon the whole village knew that we were in communication with 'abroad'.

The packages were from Papa's brother, my Uncle Wilek, and were postmarked in a place called New York, New York. This is how we learned that Uncle Wilek had reached the last stage of his odyssey from Lithuania. We already knew from Grandmother Blattberg's postcards to Kuma that he had traveled to Tokyo via Moscow and Vladivostok and, later, when we were still in Kuma before the German invasion, we received a picture postcard from Hawaii. That postcard stood propped up on an empty tea tin on a tiny shelf next to my parents' bed. The picture showed a beach in Honolulu, with a coconut tree, a garish sky and an orangey sun that looked fake. On the other side was Uncle Wilek's scribbled message: 'My dearest ones, We send you warm greetings from Honolulu, your loving Wilek.'

That card and the tea tin – a relic from more opulent times in 1943 – provided the only touches of color and exotica in our weathered *izba*. Honolulu, which in Polish is pronounced with a hard 'H' and an accent on the 'lulu', was a word that could be rolled around one's tongue a thousand times without losing its magic.

And now we had some packages from another mysterious place, New York, New York. We waited till Papa returned from work before opening them. There were a great many items of food and clothing, of which I remember only a package of sugar, a tin of Hershey's cocoa, a tin of powdered eggs and, irony of ironies, a pair of brand new children's shoes made of bicolored leather, with tips darker than the rest – just like in the ill-fated clownish shoes with the clumsy felt tips that I loathed so passionately. The powdered eggs provided my very first exposure to processed food; when mixed with water, they could be cooked to a somewhat lumpy, scrambled mass that was but distantly related to the velvety splendor of a real egg but tasted very good nevertheless.

The more I think about my childhood, the more I see that my life has evolved out of a series of minute probabilities, each one so tiny that a combination of them all provides a number which is almost infinitesimally small. By the most elementary calculation, I should be, if not long since dead, then at the very least living a totally different life in a totally different place.

At every turning point of my existence, I can play a game of 'What If?' What if Mama had not run from Mielec in September of 1939? What if I had not screamed 'Tatko! Tatko!' on the road to Lwów? What if we had not met on the Volga the Russian couple who directed us to Kambarka? What if there were no *Neftebaza* in Kambarka, with all its rich wives who could afford to buy Mama's fineries and her wedding ring, and get away with wearing them at a time when outward displays of 'bourgeois decadence', such as wedding rings, were politically incorrect? What if we had not received Uncle Wilek's packages? . . .

For the first time in about eighteen months we were able to take a tiny step back from the edge of starvation. We never received any letters from Uncle Wilek and so it was only after

1. Great-grandfather Aaron Schwarz.

2. Grandmother Estera (Erna) Schwarz Schreiber as a young woman.

3. Grandfather Abraham Schreiber with my Aunt Herminka Schreiber Diamand (pregnant with my cousin Anita) and my cousin Marcel on the left; a friend on the right. Kraków 1932.

4. Grandmother Leah (Laura) Landau Blattberg shortly before her death (from an ID photograph taken for 'Aryan' papers).

5. My Uncle Wolf (Wilek) Blattberg.

6. My mother Anna Schreiber Blattberg as a young woman.

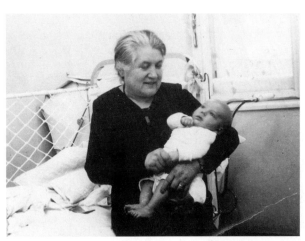

7. Grandmother Schreiber with my cousin Romek. Kraków 1935.

8. Mother (standing at the back) and friends in Zakopane.

9. My parents in late summer 1936 (my mother is pregnant with me).

10. Family vacation in Rabka. Standing, from left to right: Charles (Salo) Schwarz, Grandmother Schreiber's brother (who lived in France); Hela Oppenheim Schreiber, Uncle Menek's wife; unidentified. Sitting, from left to right: Grandmother Schreiber, my Aunt Janka Schreiber Wassertheil, Helen Schwarz (Salo's wife); unidentified. Rabka 1938.

11. Aunt Janka with my cousin Romek (Romeczek). Kraków.

12. Before the storm: with my friend Henryś Maj, a few weeks before the German invasion.

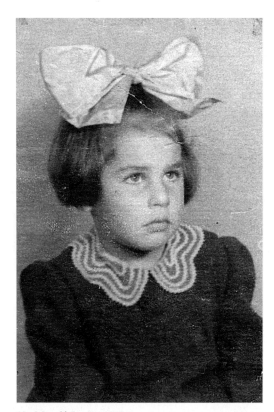

13. Myself, Lwów 1940.   14. Papa, Kambarka (1945?).

15. Telegram announcing survival of Grandmother Schreiber, Uncle Menek and Aunt Hela in Poland. The text is in broken French: Maman, Hela, moi suis santé (maman, Hela, myself am health).

16. Myself in Kraków.

17. The three Schiff brothers in our apartment on Aleja Słowackiego. From left to right: Duduś, Zelek and Kalmek.

18. The first postwar Passover *seder* in our apartment on Aleja Słowackiego. Sitting from left to right: Aunt Janka, Papa, Janka's husband Jules Wassertheil, Zelek Schiff, Mama, Uncle Menek Schreiber, his wife Hela, Kalmek Schiff. Standing: Romek and I (David (Duduś) Schiff took the photograph). Note a photograph of Grandfather Schreiber in front of Mama, and photographs of other dead relatives on the chest of drawers.

19. My cousin Marcel Diamand.

20. Myself (on the right) with my cousins Anita Diamand, Romek Wassertheil and baby Adam Schreiber.

21. Mother in 1947.

22. My parents and I, Paris 1950.

24. A postcard from Grandmother Schreiber, November 1945, from liberated Kraków.

23. Grandmother Schreiber as Elżbieta Steczowicz.

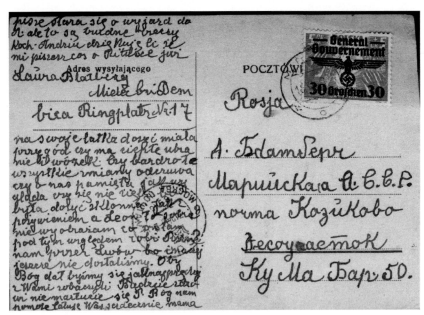

25. A postcard from Grandmother Blattberg, November 1940.

26. A postcard from Grandmother Blattberg, January 1941.

leaving Russia that we learned how he had succeeded in finding us in Kambarka through his work at the World Jewish Congress in New York. His connections there led him to the list of Polish refugees in the Soviet Union. That step was clear enough. That he persisted in sending us packages month after month, without ever receiving an acknowledgement, not knowing if even one of those packages had reached us, is also fairly easy to understand.

The real mystery lies in the timing of those packages. Why did we receive five of them all at once, why then, and why only then? The best answer to these questions, of course, is that some bureaucrat decided that it was the politically correct thing to do. The second best answer is, 'Go figure!'

Yet I am sufficiently fond of my own speculation to introduce it here. I think that we were the lucky beneficiaries of the one brief shining moment of cordial relations between the Red Army and the Western Allies: it was precisely at that time that Russian and US troops were getting ready to join forces on the Elbe River, amidst much embracing, drinking, and fraternizing.

The war was coming to an end, but there was very little joy in our house. Mama remained steadfast in her refusal to attend any celebrations or entertainment so long as she had no news of her mother. 'Entertainment' in Kambarka consisted of a projectionist who came about once a month from Izhevsk to show a movie at the meeting hall that was normally used for political education sessions. His arrival always caused a great stir among the kids in my class. I was the only one who had never seen a movie – a state of affairs that I resented bitterly. This is why, and I am embarrassed to say this, I remember the day when we learned of Grandmother Schreiber's survival mostly as the day of my first trip to the movies.

It must have been in early June of 1945, about a month after the end of the war, on a mild and sunny day. Mama and I were working in our tiny vegetable garden when the postmistress walked into our yard and drew from her battered leather satchel a telegram from Poland. Mama guessed instantly that it was good news because, as she later put it, 'dead Jews don't send telegrams', but her hands shook so violently that at first she could not read the message. Then she read it, but couldn't speak. At last she said in a small, quiet, faraway voice: '*Moja Mamusia przeżyła*' [My mammy has survived].

The telegram consisted of six strips of paper glued with messy globs of brown glue onto a yellowed piece of newspaper dating back to 1942, about the same vintage as the cut-up sheets of newspaper that were distributed to us at school in lieu of writing paper. The message was on two lines written in a foreign language that Mama later told me was broken French (she had learned a bit of French in high school).

I did not think of wondering why someone in Poland would write in French to someone living in Russia. The world of adults was so crazy that nothing was surprising. In hindsight, I suspect that the telegram must have been forwarded via some organization like the Red Cross in French-speaking Geneva. The text was: '*Maman – Hela – moi – suis – santé – écrivez*' [Mother – Hela – I – am – health – write]. Uncle Menek's name, Manuel Schreiber, came at the end, after some acronyms and the name of someone called Straszewski. Miracle of miracles, not only was Grandmother Schreiber alive, but Uncle Menek and his wife, Aunt Hela, had survived as well!

As it happened, the projectionist was in town that evening and Mama consented to take me to my first, and last, movie outing in Kambarka. Papa, perhaps already convinced in his heart of hearts that his parents were dead, stayed at home. Mama and I walked together to the meeting hall, which was at the other end of town, but Mama wasn't paying the slightest attention to me. She seemed completely oblivious of my presence. Walking so fast that I had to run to keep up with her, she was talking and gesticulating to herself. Contrary to her usual incomprehensible mutterings about Hitler, this time she was cursing him in a loud, clear voice and shouting over and over, 'May he burn in hell for ever and ever! May his dark soul never know any peace!'

This outburst terrified me because Mama, albeit often fierce in defense of me or Papa, was inherently a very gentle person who never cursed anyone. '*Niech go szlak trafi!*' [May he have a stroke!] was about as bad a curse as I was used to hearing. My vocabulary of crime, punishment and evil was limited to diffuse expressions such as 'Death to the fascists, slayers of mankind!' or 'Crush the German invaders!' And here was Hitler suddenly emerging in my head as the focus of all our misfortunes and the sole personification of Evil.

The movie was a patriotic children's story in black-and-white about an evil giant who was ravaging the land of a peace-loving people and killing thousands upon thousands of innocents. I sat there in a trance as Hitler and the evil giant melded into one and the same, even as the projector kept jamming with a shuddering noise, causing the image to jump convulsively and then literally melt. The final scene showed the defeated evil giant in his death throes. He fell to the ground with a thundering noise as the earth split beneath him and swallowed him whole. There was much applause, hooting and cheering from the audience, but I did not join in as I was still locked in my trance. The movie kept replaying in my head day after day for a very long time and, although I was glad that the evil giant was crushed, I was greatly saddened by the devastation that he had left in his wake.

7   Return to Kraków

We spent the second half of 1945 waiting for repatriation, waiting for permission to return to the country of our birth, where our ancestors had lived for generations. It was also the land where Jewish ashes lay scattered to the four winds. Yet, miraculously, Mama's nuclear family had survived – her sisters in Central Asia, her brother and her mother under the Germans. Papa was less fortunate. His parents were dead, as was almost every member of the large Blattberg clan in Mielec. Of the twelve Blattberg siblings, and their twelve spouses, only Great-aunt Sarah remained. Fewer than a handful of Papa's many cousins were alive.

And still we longed to return to this place that we called home and I still prayed to Dziadziusio Schreiber every night, imploring him to 'bring us safely back'. It was an interminable wait that was eased somewhat by our correspondence with the remnants of our family. Mail from Poland was delivered erratically, and often not at all, yet it was not forbidden to Polish nationals. This was an exceptional privilege at a time when Soviet citizens were kept incommunicado behind the walls of Fortress Russia and any Soviet person suspected of contact with 'abroad' received a 'letter of invitation' to the local NKVD quarters, or worse.

In November 1945 Grandmother Schreiber wrote: 'We have sent you the *"vyzovs"*; people are returning, completely destitute.' This sentence tells us that ex-deportees were already returning from Russia while we were still sitting in Kambarka and waiting for our exit papers, including our *'vyzovs'*. (A Russian word meaning 'invitation', a *'vyzov'* was an affidavit in which Uncle Menek vouched for us and 'invited' us back to our own country. It was one of the documents that we apparently needed in order to be allowed to return.)

Repatriation was serious business. Eligible Polish nationals were to return collectively in special trains, the famous *eshalons* that we knew only too well from our voyage in 1940. The *eshalons* from Udmurt ASSR were to leave from the regional capital of Izhevsk. Those still lacking a valid exit permit or otherwise unable to leave on the date set for departure would just have to stay behind. The gates of Fortress Russia would come down behind the *eshalons* and would not reopen for stragglers.

Exit papers for the members of the Polish community in Kambarka were handled through the local Association of Polish Patriots, the ZPP – in other words by Papa, who had been appointed President of the Kambarka ZPP, much to his despair. Papa traveled several times to Izhevsk on *komandirovka* assignments and dealt there with the NKVD officer in charge of all the exit applications from Udmurtia. That officer was a small-time potentate whose decisions could not be challenged. He was apparently also a rather jovial man who liked his vodka and was not above drinking in his office, even going so far as to offer Papa a glass or two. Though he loathed the taste of vodka, and did not feel like celebrating, Papa dutifully raised his glass in a toast to Polish–Soviet friendship and swallowed in a single gulp. Over our years in Kambarka, he had learned the hard way that refusing to join in the ritual of drinking would be construed as a sign of disrespect for his host and an appalling lack of manhood.

By January of 1946 Papa had secured exit papers for all the Polish citizens in Kambarka, with the exception of two families: one whose name I cannot remember and the other – ours.

Its name notwithstanding, the ZPP was a creation of Moscow and did Moscow's bidding. When it appeared that Papa, the president of the local ZPP, had done or said something that made him *persona non grata* with the NKVD (I was never told what it was) we were punished through denial of our exit papers. The prospect of staying behind in Kambarka, at the mercy of the NKVD and once again deprived of contact with our family in Kraków, was terrifying. My parents were so distressed that they completely forgot to celebrate my ninth birthday.

About two or three weeks after my uncelebrated birthday, Papa had secured everyone's exit papers but ours. The first *eshalon* from Udmurtia was already standing at the railway station in Izhevsk and was scheduled to leave within the next few days. However, most of the Poles from Kambarka were supposed to wait a few weeks longer for a second *eshalon* that would depart in March. Our trunk was already packed but, alas, it seemed that we were doomed to remain in Kambarka while all the other Poles were getting ready to leave for Izhevsk with their bundles. It is difficult to describe my parents' feelings of despair and helplessness after everyone left in mid-March. Papa went with them on a final *komandirovka* assignment, but Mama and I had to stay in our *izba* because we had no exit papers, not even a travel permit from Kambarka to Izhevsk. Our last hopes were now pinned on the NKVD officer in charge of exit applications, whom Papa was supposed to see for some last-minute signatures on behalf of the group already on its way to the *eshalon*. Papa was planning to make the NKVD man mellow with a generous offering of vodka and then unobtrusively slip our own unsigned exit papers among the documents that still awaited signature. It was a desperate ploy that could easily backfire, but we were now at the eleventh hour and had little to lose. Papa left for the 135-kilometer journey to Izhevsk, telling us to be ready to leave in an instant if by good fortune he should return with our exit papers properly signed and stamped.

Mama and I had our trunk packed. Bread and other supplies for the journey were tied in a bundle and ready to be picked up instantly. With the *eshalon* about to leave within two or three days, we were engaged in an almost hopeless race against the clock because the trip to and from Izhevsk took a long time, as the trains were few and their schedules erratic. Furthermore, the Kambarka railway station was about six kilometers away – a distance that was often impossible on foot in winter weather. We were fortunate in that our friends the Totcholovskis were standing by, ready at any moment to take us to the station in a sleigh. Mr Totcholovski, who was an influential man in town, had also promised to help get us on a train to Izhevsk, even one seemingly off-limits to civilians.

A whole day passed, and then a second one. Another evening came and Papa had still not returned. Mama and I spent the night sitting on our packed trunk by the window. We did not speak. There was nothing to say, as we both knew that we had very little hope of reaching the *eshalon* in time even if Papa managed to return with our exit papers. We were grieving for ourselves and for sweet, gentle Tamara Nun, who lay dying of pneumonia. At the age of fifteen, Tamara was now a Komsomol,[1] a young Communist, and she had been called upon to help clear the snow from railway tracks after a recent snowfall. Even Mr Nun's pull at the *Neftebaza* could not exempt a Komsomol from doing her patriotic duty. Tamara had been sent to clear snow with a sore throat and a racking cough, and now she lay dying of pneumonia.

I was silently praying to Dziadziusio Schreiber, notwithstanding his manifest failure to protect most of our family in the past. 'Please, Dziadziusio, please,' I begged him, 'please make Tamara live, please make Papa come with our exit papers right now and bring us safely back home to Kraków!'

It was very cold inside our *izba*. Mama and I were huddled on our trunk, holding onto each other for warmth and for solace. Mama did not sleep at all while I dozed on and off. It was still dark when I awoke with a start: Papa was knocking on the window. We could plainly see his silhouette, outlined against the white backdrop of the snow. He was triumphantly waving a piece of paper, our exit papers!

The vodka bribery plot had been successful, though not exactly as planned. Papa had grossly underestimated the NKVD officer's talent for downing glass after glass without losing control. Although quite tipsy, the NKVD man knew exactly what he was doing. He separated our papers from the rest of the file and waved them under Papa's nose. '*Nu, ty absolutno chotchiesh iz naszei rodiny uyezzhat!*' [So, you want absolutely to leave our Motherland!] he roared, using the derogatory form of 'you', the one used to address an inferior. He spent an interminable minute playing cat-and-mouse with Papa, making him believe that he was going to rip up our papers. At last he yelled, '*Ciort z toboi!*' [Go to the devil!], and signed.

Papa was able to squeeze into a train for Kambarka and

then he trudged the six kilometers from the station in his *lapcies* stuffed with old newspapers. He hadn't eaten in a day and was faint with hunger. Mama gave him some bread from our bundle of supplies for the journey. There was no time for a meal. The *eshalon* was scheduled to leave Izhevsk in the afternoon and only a miracle would bring us there in time. Mama ran to wake up the Totcholovskis. We said goodbye to our *izba* while waiting for their sleigh. It stopped in front of our house in the morning stillness, the last moment of calm before our frenzied race from Kambarka.

We dashed to the schoolhouse and waited in the sleigh while Papa ran inside to let the principal know that we were leaving. He came back after a few minutes, holding my report card in his hand. I still have that tiny piece of paper with the stamp of the school and the date of our departure: March 20, 1946.

We dashed to the station. To our absolute dismay, the station employee informed us that there was no passenger train bound for Izhevsk that morning and that the next freight train was not scheduled to stop in Kambarka. Mr Totcholovski took the employee to the side and the two men held a whispered conversation. After waiting on the platform for what seemed like an eternity, we heard a train approaching from a distance. It was the freight train that was not supposed to stop in Kambarka. The station employee ran to the switching area and flagged the train to an unscheduled stop. There was a row of sealed boxcars followed by about a dozen open-bed cars heaped with coal. The Totcholovskis helped us to climb onto one of the open cars and to hoist our trunk there. We nestled at the bottom of a pyramid of coal chunks that were partially covered with snow in a speckled black-and-white pattern which reminded me of our chicken Pepitko. We hugged and thanked the Totcholovskis and waved goodbye to them when the train started to move.

We kept waving goodbye for as long as we could distinguish their silhouettes on the platform. We knew that if we reached the *eshalon* in time we would never again see this warm-hearted couple who helped us in our hour of need out of pure generosity and risked their own safety by helping us, for Papa was now suspect in the eyes of the NKVD. 'How are we ever going to repay them?' Mama sighed. For many years after leaving Kambarka, Mama kept regretting that she could not send even a token gift to these devoted friends, or at least write to them and find out how they were faring. We never heard from anyone who remained in Kambarka. We never learned whether Tamara Nun found the strength to recover from pneumonia, nor how Diedushko was getting by, or the good Tatar woman who had lost all her four children at the Front. We were leaving a town whose atmosphere was quintessentially Russian: chaotic, unpredictable, a mixture of warm empathy and random cruelty. Yet when I look back now from the perspective of a lifetime, especially after my encounter with the brutish antisemitic hatred of postwar Poland, it is the warmth and the empathy of those simple people that I remember above all else.

Huddled on our open heap of coal, we were freezing. The wind was howling and a light snow had started to fall. Mama was not looking well; she had a cold, she was coughing and she seemed feverish. The freight train was moving excruciatingly slowly. With each minute that passed, our hope of reaching the *eshalon* before its departure from Izhevsk became slimmer and slimmer, but I was so cold, and my hands and my feet hurt so much, that I was beyond caring. When we reached the Izhevsk station in the early afternoon we were so numb and stiff that we had great trouble climbing down from the freight car. Papa thought that he knew where the *eshalon* was standing, but it had been moved to a different siding overnight and we wasted precious time looking for it. We wasted even more time while our papers were repeatedly checked by NKVD guards.

We were on the right platform at last. Our papers were checked again. The train was about to pull away from the station but we were not able to climb aboard because the doors of the boxcars near us were already closed. A guard was rushing us toward a car that still stood open. The door was located at a forbidding height and I could not reach up to it. The guard was yelling, '*Bystro! Bystro! Davai!*' [Hurry! Hurry! Move it!] Some arms extended toward us and pulled me and Mama into the car while Papa was shoving our trunk behind us and the guard was pushing him inside. We could feel the wheels rumbling below our feet, the sliding door of the car slammed shut and the train began gathering speed. The *eshalon* was leaving Izhevsk and we were inside the *eshalon*.

The terror of that day in Izhevsk engulfs me every time someone exclaims about catching a plane or making a connection 'by the skin of my teeth'. How fortunate are they, who do not know the real meaning of that phrase! As for me, I can still hear the echo of our frenzied race to the open boxcar. If we had been delayed for a few seconds more we would have remained behind, locked up for good inside a postwar Soviet Union that was sealed from the world for the next ten years. While it is true that several thousand Polish citizens were released in 1956, during the Krushchevian period of 'thaw' in relations with the West, I do not think that we would have been among them. Had we returned to Kambarka, my father would most probably have been arrested for 'anti-Soviet' activities and my mother, who had no profession and whose health was deteriorating, would probably have died of malnutrition or disease, and I would have been sent to some Udmurt orphanage.

But on that afternoon in Izhevsk, as the door of the boxcar was sliding shut behind us, my only thought was for my wildly racing heart that was trying to leap out of my chest. When it calmed down, I saw that we were in a standard Soviet *tieplushka*: a boxcar where tiers of wooden bunks were arrayed on all sides and a small space in the middle was kept free for use as a common area heated by a cast-iron stove. All the bunks but four were occupied. We were shown to three unused bunks in a corner and it soon became obvious why there was no one there. There was a large hole, as big as several fists, in the wall of the car between the two lower bunks, and there was a hole almost as big just above the topmost bunk. The heat emanating from the little cast-iron stove in the middle of the *tieplushka* never reached our remote corner, and the wind kept howling through the gaps despite all our efforts at plugging them. Snow and ice mysteriously found their way into my bedding. One English-speaking jester among our fellow passengers nicknamed our boxcar corner the *Wuthering Heights*. He very kindly recounted for me the plot of Emily Brontë's book. As I had already more or less read *Hamlet*, I concluded that English literature specialized in stories of gloom and doom.

We traveled in our *tieplushka* for several weeks, mostly standing idle at side-tracks in order to make room for regularly scheduled trains. Every type of train appeared to have priority over us, including what looked like military convoys heading east. Sealed cars alternated with open flat-top carriages that were loaded with massive objects concealed by tarpaulins. The Soviets were supposedly still bringing back war spoils from Germany. The defeated Germans were said to be completely destitute, which 'was more than they deserved anyway, may they all burn in hell for all eternity'. As for the sealed cars, they were allegedly filled with convicts bound for the gulags, perhaps German prisoners of war, but most likely Russian soldiers who had crossed over into the Western sectors of occupied Germany and whom the Western Allies had handed back to the Soviets.

This incident remains vividly etched in my mind, probably because it was the first time that I heard a politically charged conversation freely carried out in the open, but otherwise I remember almost nothing of those weeks, not even our fellow passengers. My world was reduced to its essence, and distilled into that essence was the dread of losing my mother. Mama had left Kambarka with a cough that became worse during our journey on the open coal heap and had now turned into pneumonia. For an endless ten days, she struggled for her life on her freezing bunk, without any oxygen or any medicine. Our fellow passengers tried to help but could not do very much. Papa was nursing Mama day and night but I just sat on my bunk and breathed with each one of Mama's tortured breaths, and held my breath when she seemed to stop breathing. For the first time in my life, no one cared whether my hands were clean or my hair properly braided, or even whether I had eaten. I was plunged into the depths of a black abyss where nothing was of any importance.

And then a miracle happened. One morning as I was standing by the stove to warm my always freezing hands, I saw that Mama was trying to talk to me. I ran toward her bunk. 'Don't stand so close to the stove, you could get burned if the train starts suddenly,' she whispered. Mama was nagging me once more! She was better! She was no longer delirious! What she said even made sense because a woman in our *tieplushka* had been severely burned when a kettle of boiling water fell on her leg as the train lurched to a stop. Mama remained very weak and bedridden, but she was breathing more freely and she was up and around a few days before the *eshalon* arrived at its terminus in Lódz.

The journey from Lódz to Kraków was yet another nightmare. We bought train tickets with money that Uncle Menek had sent us to Kambarka and we showed up at the departure platform for Kraków with plenty of time to spare, naively expecting to climb aboard. Little did we know that throngs of people, many of them thuggish-looking young men, would take the cars by storm, leaving behind the weak and the unfit. We were kicked and shoved away from two trains during the daylight hours. Luckily for us, we had not yet heard of the armed NSZ[2] gangs who specialized in killing Jews inside and outside of trains, and so were not overly terrified. Scared, hungry, and utterly exhausted, we finally managed to muscle our way into a night train that was filled with a slightly less menacing crowd of passengers. We were so densely packed that, when she fainted from exhaustion, Mama had nowhere to fall and she remained standing, unconscious, until Papa revived her. We were backed into a corner where Mama and Papa were shielding me with their bodies so that I would not get trampled. I was nearly crushed to death when a scuffle suddenly erupted in our vicinity and there was a violent reshuffling of angry torsos and elbows. It was Mama who shielded me with her emaciated body and found the superhuman strength required to push away a heavy man who was smothering me.

We arrived at Kraków Główny, the central railway station located in the heart of the city, at five or six o'clock in the morning, when it was still dark outside. It was but a short walk to Grandmother's apartment house at number 15 Batory Street. Unfortunately, the elevator in her building was not working and Mama, who had exhausted every particle of her strength during our journey from Lódz, was unable to walk up the five endless flights of stairs. Papa was forced to help her at every step.

A few minutes after we rang the doorbell, Uncle Menek cautiously opened the door. We were standing in an enormous circular entrance hall with doors all around it. A figure dressed in a blue robe came through a door directly opposite the entrance. It was Grandmother. We all stood frozen to the floor and looked silently at one another across the vast hallway. At last Grandmother said, *'Ja się doczekałam.'* [I have lived to see this day.]

Mama, who was the first to move, began walking in slow motion in the direction of Grandmother, but her legs would not carry her and she had to crawl over the polished floor. Grandmother lifted her to her feet. Mama was so light that even an old lady could pick her up. Mama said, *'Mamusiu, o mamusiu!'* in a small, soft voice that held within it the entire story of the past six years. Suddenly, they were all embracing, Mama, Papa, Grandmother, Uncle Menek, Aunt Hela; embracing and sobbing, embracing and sobbing, embracing and sobbing.

Soon I too was engulfed in their arms. Unlike Mama, who was feverish and gaunt, Grandmother was plump and soft. She wore a thin flannel robe of a pale blue color, printed with forget-me-nots of a darker blue and some tiny white flowers. The fabric was wet with tears.

They were all exclaiming how tall I was, and how pale, and how thin, and in need of fattening up. They led us through a long corridor to an enormous kitchen where I ate a huge breakfast. Aunt Hela brought in my little cousin Adaś, who was about twelve months old – the child of hope and survival, conceived in defiance of all odds when the Germans had not yet retreated. He was screaming: a plump infant with brown eyes, nothing very interesting. *'Kaneine hore!'* Mama and Papa both exclaimed with admiration. And someone added: *'Am Israel chai'* [The people of Israel lives].

Except for cooing to Adaś, no one said very much. How was one to speak about the last six years? Who was going to recite the names of all those who were missing? Tears were streaming silently down Grandmother's face. A few were falling onto her robe with the blue forget-me-nots that was already wet with all our mingled tears. Mama was too weak to eat and drank only a little warm milk. She was more dead than alive. Her fierce willpower and her intense yearning for her mother had sustained her thus far, but now she was completely drained. She was put to bed in one of the many rooms of that huge apartment, where a bed was also installed for Papa.

Mama had recurring pneumonia. Her life hung in the balance for weeks even after Uncle Menek managed to procure some sulfamide antibiotics, then a priceless medicine that was smuggled in from the American occupation zone in Germany.

Nobody was answering any of my questions about Mama. It was a period of time when grown-ups were convinced that they were doing children a great favor by keeping from them all the bad news. It was called '*obronić dziecko*' [to shield the child]. Did they really think that I had no eyes to see or ears to overhear, nor a galloping imagination? The doctor and our few surviving friends and relatives kept calling every day. Hiding in the nooks and crannies of that vast apartment, it was not hard for me to overhear bits of ominous conversations: 'The doctor is not optimistic. He says it's a miracle how she has managed to survive that trip,' and 'her poor lungs are ruined,' and 'it all goes back to those horrible attacks of malaria in Kuma.'

I was desperately clinging to Grandmother, hanging onto her apron as if I could magically make up for those six lost years. I did not yet know that she had a serious heart condition and that we would lose her before the year was out. I saw that she was moving very slowly and sitting down very often, but to me her very slowness was part and parcel of her comforting presence – I had a grandmother, and grand-mothers were supposed to be old.

She wore a big apron over a dress of black crêpe de chine decorated with a collar of creamy lace. She baked for me some cookies that I had never even dreamt of: luscious meringues made with egg whites and sugar. She showed me how to beat the egg whites and the sugar with a whisk until the slimy egg transformed into satiny peaks that were gleaming like pearls.

We used the yolks to make a 'gogel-mogel', a concoction made of egg yolk and sugar that was supposed to help Mama regain her strength. But Mama was not hungry. She was too exhausted. She sipped a little bit of Grandmother's delicious chicken broth and fell back on her pillow.

I made such a nuisance of myself that Grandmother let me sleep in her bed – an arrangement that we both regretted yet pretended to enjoy. I kept waking Grandmother up by thrashing around in the bed, and she added to my nightmares by screaming in the middle of the night. She screamed, '*O Jezus-Maria, O rany boskie!*' [O Jesus and Mary, O wounds of God!]

Come morning she was again herself, Estera Erna Schreiber, my Jewish grandmother, but at night she was haunted by Elżbieta Steczowicz, the Polish countrywoman whose persona she had adopted under the occupation. Grandmother had been able to pass for an Aryan because she was blond and blue-eyed and had a broad Slavic face. She also knew how to speak like a countrywoman, thanks to her many years of living among the countryfolk of Tymbark, but she had to drill herself relentlessly in order to absorb the proper way of saying '*O Jezus-Maria*', of making the sign of the cross and behaving in church. The strain was enormous, since she felt responsible for the lives of Uncle Menek and Aunt Hela as well as her own, lest a suspicious Pole denounce them all, and she still had nightmares more than eighteen months after their liberation.

Roaming the streets of my native city over the next few weeks, I soon learned much more about the face of Polish Catholicism than just the proper way of exclaiming '*O Jezus-Maria.*'

Kraków was a magnificent city, virtually unscathed by the war. The soul-pleasing sound of church bells resonated everywhere. The beautiful Mariacki church, where a hauntingly mournful tune was played on top of the tower once every hour, was but a short walk away. Around the corner from our house was Karmelicka Ulica, the street of the Carmelite convent and numerous churches. Electric streetcars were rumbling slowly up and down the street. Every passer-by and every streetcar rider was making the sign of the cross in front of every church, everyone but I, the little Jewess who had 'betrayed Our Savior and condemned Him to the cross'.

I was so naive and bewildered that it took me some time to understand what was happening, but when at last I noticed the murderous stares of the passers-by a chill went down my spine like a knife. And I shall never forget the instant when a streetcar stopped momentarily in front of a church because of some traffic disturbance. I met the eyes of an older boy who was sitting inside the tram, his leering face glued to the window. The eyes were full of hatred. When the tram lurched away a few seconds later, a horrible thing happened. The boy lifted his chin with one of his hands, and with his other hand he made a quick slashing gesture across his own exposed throat. There was absolutely no way to misunderstand the meaning of that gesture. It was the very same, I later learned, that Poles had often made during the war while watching columns of Jews being marched to their death. Welcome home, little girl from Kambarka!

I was the product of an atheistic Soviet society where being Jewish, albeit something not entirely healthy, was not viewed as a threat and a disease. Nothing in my previous experience had prepared me for my encounter with Catholic Poland, and it was a measure of the disarray in my family that during my mother's illness I was left to wander in Kraków entirely on my own at a time when Jews were still being murdered.

In this royal capital, the heart of Polish intellectual tradition, the seat of the proud Jagiellonian University, many were still convinced – nay, they fervently believed – that Jews were using the blood of Christian children for ritual purposes. The first pogrom in postwar Poland took place not in some remote village but in Kraków, on August 11, 1945, when a frenzied mob stormed the Kupa synagogue on Miodowa street in search of 'the corpses of Christian children who had been drained of their blood'.

Great-aunt Sarah, who was in Kraków at the time, wrote in her memoir of yet another incident: 'One time, I was in the street with my daughter when a mob of hooligans appeared, yelling "Kill Jews!" We managed to escape with our lives in a streetcar. At this time, the Polish enemies killed a Jewish couple who had survived Hitler's hell.'

One of the most frightening things that happened in our

house soon after our return to Kraków was Papa's trip to Mielec, where he went in order to inquire about the fate of his family. Since many Jews had been murdered after the war when they came back to reclaim their possessions, Papa made it perfectly clear in Mielec that he had no intention of reclaiming anything at all. Besides, the estate at Gliny Wielkie had been expropriated by the communist regime. As for the house at Rynek 17, Great-aunt Sarah had promised it to the family of Jozef Mądry, the Polish peasant who had saved her and one of her two daughters, and Papa respected her wishes. Yet he was nearly killed by his former neighbors. He wouldn't tell me anything about his trip, except for repeating, '*Kindleben*, you don't know how lucky I am to be here alive!' And he was hugging me very hard, something that he never did when he was in his normal state.

Later, when he had to go to Warsaw to apply for our exit visas, Papa refused to take the train for fear of being murdered by NSZ thugs, a perfectly reasonable fear under the circumstances. Instead, he spent a bundle of our precious money, the money that we were saving penny by penny in order to get a new start in the West, on a plane ticket to the capital.

Shortly thereafter, I went back to school, a neighborhood public school. A crucifix hung in every classroom, and by then I had learned to be afraid of the cross. Classes in religious instruction were taught by a young priest in a long black cassock. The three Jewish children in my class, myself and two other girls, were excused from participating but we were required to sit at the back of the room during the lessons. The priest was a gentle, mild-mannered man who tolerated our whispering and giggling so long as we did not cause a disturbance. Once, in a gesture of defiance, we sat noisily chomping on bread and sausage in the middle of a lesson about the Holy Trinity, but the priest, to his credit, chose to ignore our rudeness, of which I am still vaguely ashamed.

I was naive to the point of stupidity. One morning during history lesson, our teacher, Mrs Zakszewska, called for the year of Poland's conversion to Christianity, the year of *Chrzest Polski*, a date by which the country defines itself and marks its true beginning. Not a single Catholic hand was raised, yet I foolishly raised mine.

Mrs Zakszewska was beside herself. 'How stupid can you all be?' she screamed. 'Nobody knows the date of *Chrzest Polski*! Only this little Jew-girl knows!' she continued, pointing her finger at me as if to make sure that nobody would forget who I was. She went on ranting for some time before the class resumed.

I could not help being a good student because I loved learning. My grades were very good and, one fine day, my name was posted on the honor roll in the entrance hall. The next day, it was gone and two of my grades were lowered without explanation, still good but not good enough for my name to appear on the honor roll. My parents did not even bother going to complain.

A few days later, my two Jewish classmates and I were running in the school yard during recess. All of a sudden, I was surrounded by a group of older children who tripped me and pushed me to the ground. The courtyard was covered with exceedingly sharp pebbles which made ugly gashes in both of my knees. I still have the scars from that day. I lay there stunned for some time. My two Jewish classmates were afraid to help me because the older children were still surrounding me. Two teachers who were supposed to keep order during recess watched without lifting a finger. I hobbled away at last with the help of an older girl, a do-gooder who was a Girl Scout.

'Why are you helping this repulsive, mangy Jew-girl?' a child asked her.

She answered, 'Because I am a Girl Scout and the Girl Scout code commands me to look after plants and animals.'

I had at last found my rightful place in Polish society.

8 Under the General-gouvernement

There was so much pain, so much grieving, quiet and unspoken but so palpable that even a nine-year-old child could feel its crushing weight. We had all returned from hiding or from Russia only to be confronted by hostility, hatred, greed, and even envy. Why anyone would envy people who had lost their families, their homes, their possessions, and their way of life was an utter mystery, but envy there was – for the jobs that we were purportedly stealing and the caches of gold that we were all said to have.

For the most part, the adults coped with their grief through silence. The vocabulary of survival had not yet been invented: 'holocaust' and 'shoah' were just words in a dictionary; they had nothing to do with us. And had one mentioned a phrase such as 'grief counseling' or 'support group', one would have been considered a lunatic. Grown-ups simply went about the routine of daily living, of rebuilding shattered lives, of applying for emigration.

But grief is bound to surface. On the first Passover *seder* that we celebrated together – it was in 1947 and Grandmother Schreiber was already dead – a river of tears flowed on the festive table. Zelek Schiff, who was reading the Haggada, broke down first and instantly all the grown-ups began sobbing uncontrollably. Women took out handkerchiefs that were tucked in their sleeves, men took handkerchiefs out of a pocket, and everyone just sat there crying, not saying anything, thinking of all the *seders* that their fathers had led and their mothers prepared, of their little brothers who had asked the *kashot*, and of all the little children who had been running around searching for the *afikoimen*. And, as I look back on that evening now, I see that, though the oldest of the *seder* guests was only in his forties, not one adult in that room had a mother or a father. The entire generation of elders had been wiped out.

Until her death at the beginning of December 1946, Grandmother Shreiber had been the sole surviving grandparent in our once extended circle of relatives and friends. Grandmother, Uncle Menek and Aunt Hela survived because they had escaped from Lwów shortly after the June 1941 invasion. They were able to acquire 'Aryan' identity papers under the names of Elżbieta, Edward and Helena Steczowicz. In 1941 and 1942 they lived in the vicinity of Wisnicz. 'Edward Steczowicz' worked as a forester. His blond looks and his forestry experience from his childhood in Tymbark served him well. Grandmother could also easily pass for a peasant, but it has never been clear to me how they managed to pretend that Aunt Hela, a city-bred woman with a slightly semitic look, was a Polish country girl.

One of his co-workers once cornered Menek in the forest and threatened to report him to the Germans. 'I suspected that you are Jewish for some time already but now I am sure of it,' the Pole told him.

'Nonsense! And I am going to prove it to you,' Menek bluffed in a split-second while pretending to undo the first button of his fly. (Poles were never circumcised and all Jews were.)

The Pole, taken aback by my uncle's aplomb, became confused. 'No need to do that, no need, I believe you, please forget about all this,' he said.

Nevertheless, the Schreibers felt that it would be safer to move away from the Wisnicz area. They traveled on foot under cover of night. Grandmother, who had a weak heart, had trouble walking even under the best of circumstances. Uncle Menek ended up carrying her on his back across a long stretch of forest until they reached a railway station at a safe distance from Wisnicz.

In 1943, and until their liberation in September of 1944, they lived in a village near Krosno, in south-eastern Poland. Once again, a co-worker became suspicious and began blackmailing my uncle, this time for money. Luckily, Menek was aware that the blackmailer was himself vulnerable: he and some cronies were falsifying production records at the sawmill and selling truckloads of wood on the black market. Menek told the man, 'If you denounce me, the Germans will kill me, but not before

I tell them of your little scheme. And they will shoot you first.' The man immediately backed off because black-marketeering in a forest that was managed for the benefit of the Wehrmacht was an offense punishable by death. It is a miracle that the black-marketeer and his cronies did not simply murder my uncle in the forest. They must have realized that Menek, a very skillful worker, would be missed at the sawmill, and they wanted no part in a police inquiry coming too close to them.

The village near Krosno was located in an area where in 1944 the Soviet–German front frequently shifted back and forth for several endless months. One or two months into the fighting, Zelek Schwarz, a cousin whom Mama loved as a brother – her beloved Zeluś – staggered into the Steczowiczes' hut, acutely ill with a bleeding stomach ulcer. He too had been living on Aryan papers in a nearby village, and he too was forced to run from a Polish denouncer. Grandmother kept Zelek hidden behind a large armoire during the day because peasant women would often stop by unexpectedly for interminable chats. Zeluś died behind the large armoire during one of those visits, choking on his own blood in order to protect Grandmother from discovery. He died barely a week before liberation.

Grandmother, Aunt Hela and Uncle Menek returned to Kraków on April 10, 1945. My baby cousin Adaś was born ten days later. Still calling himself Edward Steczowicz, Menek managed to find a decent job and a large apartment on Basztowa street, in the heart of the city. He located us in Kambarka and helped us to return to Kraków.

On the morning of our return in the spring of 1946, Grandmother said to us, '*Ja się doczekałam*' [I have lived to see this day]. She lived for a few more months, to see her two older daughters when they returned from Central Asia, first Aunt Janka and then Aunt Herminka. Once she had enfolded to her bosom the last of all her children and grandchildren, Grandmother lost her will to live and died of congestive heart failure.

She was buried in the small Jewish cemetery on Miodowa street. Her grave is still there, undisturbed, the only family grave remaining in Poland. We could not locate Grandfather Schreiber's grave among the ruins of his cemetery. Mama said that his tombstone was among the thousands that the Germans had used to pave the access road to the slave-labor camp of Plashów.

Grandfather and Grandmother Blattberg had no grave. Only their house at Rynek 17 remained, though it had been taken over by several Polish families. Papa never spoke of Mielec, nor could he bring himself to utter his parents' names. When his first granddaughter was born, we gave her the Hebrew name of Leah, in memory of his mother. Even then, he said nothing. He did not say, 'It is good that you have given your daughter my mother's Hebrew name.' He said absolutely nothing. Were it not for Mama, even the memory of the Blattbergs in Mielec would have died – Hitler's ultimate victory.

Mama never sat me down to tell the gruesome story of Mielec, but she mentioned the Blattbergs time and again in casual conversation. One day, pointing to a small, irregularly shaped birthmark on my left upper-arm, she exclaimed, 'Do you know how extraordinary this is? Your Grandmother Blattberg had the exact same birthmark in the exact same spot!'

On another occasion she mentioned that one of Papa's aunts, Ciocia Hannah, had been living 'on Aryan papers' and working for the Polish underground resistance. Ciocia Hannah was caught by the Germans and executed in the Rynek. Her last words before she was shot in the square were, '*Niech żyje Polska!*' [Long live Poland!]

On yet another day Mama told me that one of Papa's uncles (regretfully, I cannot remember which one) was also executed in the Rynek, but as a Jew and not as a Pole. He was hanged by the feet and his body was left hanging on the square for several days.

Little by little, over the years, by listening and by reading, I have pieced together for myself an image of what happened in the *shtetl* of Mielec under the German occupation. The first massacre of Mielec Jews took place on September 13, the eve of Rosh Hashana, barely a few days after Mama and I fled to the east in our horse-driven wagon. The Germans herded Jews whom they took from the street into the main synagogue and two neighboring prayer houses. They drove 35 naked men from the communal bathhouse into the ritual slaughterhouse, where there were already women who had brought chickens to be killed for the holiday meal. Everyone was burned alive, except for those who tried to escape and who were shot.

Large-scale massacres ceased after this initial horror and, as the area was transferred to joint Wehrmacht and civilian authority and 'order' was restored, the Jews of Mielec, by and large, convinced themselves that the Erev Rosh Hashana tragedy was the work of 'isolated bands' rather than part and parcel of a systematic extermination policy. Besides, they were sure that the British and the French would defeat the Germans in a hurry. In the meantime, the suffering and the indignities – forced-labor gangs, slave labor, random killings, the armband with the Star of David, expropriations, hunger, extortionary taxation – all had to be endured until the day of deliverance. Everywhere in Poland, the Jews seem to have succumbed to this collective delusion, even well after 1939, even after several hundred thousand had died by mid-1941, during the initial period of massacres and persecution which preceded the death camps. Perhaps it is just as well, perhaps it was a sort of merciful anesthesia. Had they been fully aware of their impending death, there is almost nothing they could have done to save themselves. The Jews of Poland were completely isolated, and totally abandoned by the world.

There were about 4,000 Jews in Mielec. Their ranks swelled rapidly, and almost doubled, with the arrival of Jews who had been expelled, or who took refuge, from elsewhere. There was no ghetto in the *shtetl*. My grandparents lived in their house on Rynek 17, although they probably shared their apartment with a number of refugees. However, they must have been evicted later in 1941, along with the other Jews who lived in the better houses in the center of town.

Between May and December 1940, a number of Mielec Jews were deported for slave labor, to build fortifications on the Russian border. Five hundred Mielec Jews were deported in January of 1942. Then, on March 9 of that year, the SS and the Polish Navy-Blue Police carried out an *Aktion* [operation] that was to distinguish Mielec as the first Polish town to be declared *Judenrein* [cleansed of Jews]. As Jews were being assembled in the Rynek, the SS began removing the young men and marching them to the slave-labor camp of Pustków, located at a distance of some ten kilometers, or to Cyranka-Berdechów, a labor camp about seven kilometers away. All the others, including the old and the sick, were forced to walk the seven kilometers to Berdechów.

Berdechów had a military airfield with a huge hangar that had been built by the Polish government for an airplane factory located within an industrial zone called *Centralny Okręg Przemysłowy* (COP) [Central Industrial District]. The Polish Navy-Blues were sent back at the gates of the airfield and the rest of the *Aktion* was carried out by the Gestapo. Many elderly people were shot on the first day and buried in a mass grave by a work detail from the camp at Cyranka. The rest were herded into the COP hangar, while selections and executions continued until March 15. Meanwhile, transports proceeded to the 'Lublinland' area and from there to the death camp of Belzec.

Grandmother Blattberg died in Auschwitz with her sister Gusta. I do not know how she ended up there, since most Mielecers were transported to Belzec. But I do know that my father's young cousin Bracha Blattberg, who was a teenager at the time, was also sent to Auschwitz. She was one of the young women forced from there into the infamous 'death march' to Germany in 1945. She was liberated by the Americans and spent a year in a Swedish hospital. She now lives in Miami with her family.

I was told that Grandmother Blattberg need not necessarily have died. My Uncle Menek, who himself was hiding on 'Aryan papers', apparently managed to procure an 'Aryan' ID card for Grandmother, but she refused to leave her sister and both women died together.

Overall, the survival statistics for the large Blattberg clan in Mielec fit the roughly 1.7 per cent rate of survival for Polish Jews under the Germans. Of the many Blattberg siblings, only my Great-aunt Sarah, whom we all affection-ately called Ciocia Ucia, survived. To my knowledge, the only family member who died of natural death was my Grandfather Leib – if one can call death from a broken heart 'natural'. Grandfather became so despondent following

June 1941 – when he lost all contact with us and Uncle Wilek – that he let himself die of grief, spending his days gazing vacantly at the Rynek.

I was two-and-a-half when I saw my grandparents for the last time. It seems that Grandmother Laura and I had a special relationship, *parce que c'était elle, parce que c'était moi* [because it was she, because it was I]. She called me '*śliczniutka, słodziutka*', an untranslatable term of endearment meaning something like 'the pretty little one, the sweet little one', and I called her 'Babuniu Blattbereczek'. She would clap her hands for joy when we came to visit. She treated me with a sort of reverence. She would gently touch my cheeks and then kiss the fingers that had brushed me, like a pious Jew might kiss the fringe of his prayer shawl that had touched the Torah scrolls.

She was happy to see me even after I caused her untold embarrassment by refusing to kiss an elderly great-great-aunt. Summoned to explain why I would not give a kiss to Great-great-auntie, I apparently said, '*Bo starych ludzi się nie lubi*' [Because old people are not liked]. Unable to believe that a two-year-old would make such a preposterous statement without parroting it in some way, Great-great-auntie stormed off in a huff. The echo of this family quarrel persisted well into the war. 'I heard that Ritusia is helping with the housechores. You'll have much satisfaction from this little gossip,' writes Grandmother's sister Gusta Gretzer in November of 1940, no doubt referring to my wagging tongue.

There is no image before my eyes to celebrate the memory of Grandfather Leib. He appears to have been a modest, soft-spoken man who left no lasting impression on Mama, my primary source of information. I discovered him recently through two postcards that survived, and that he wrote to Kuma in November 1940 and February 1941.

The cards are scrawled in Gothic script, to fool the censor – it was forbidden to write in Yiddish – but many of the words are in Yiddish, beginning with the heartwrenching '*Liebe meine Kinderleben*' [Dear beloved children of my life]. Although the scrawl is huge, it is almost impossible to decipher, but I did not interpolate any of the missing words. There is no need.

The loving soul of that simple man, who still believed in God, sings to me just the same.

Mielec, November 4, 1940

Dear beloved children of my life! We are praised be God in good health. How goes it for you there? What is the sweet child Ritusia doing? What kind of work do you have there? Do you have enough to eat there? You should not worry about us, the main thing is that you stay healthy. We receive news often. We receive letters from Lemberg, but so far nothing directly from you. How is dear Andzia? You should... be sparing of your health. Wilek writes often. I greet and kiss you all from my heart... and the dear beloved Ritusia, your father

Leib Blattberg

Mielec February 9, 1941

Dear beloved children of my life, We were so very glad to receive your letter... are you... the dear Ritusie... may God grant us... we shall see each other again. How is it with you with the food and with the cold?... until God willing in good health... and Ritusie and Andzie and what kind of work are you assigned there? We think about you constantly, that we may meet again. I greet and kiss you from my heart, your father

Leib Blattberg

9 Like Leaves in the Wind

Our greatest worry is only about the position that the children find themselves in. That which has befallen us we could still endure if only we could shield the children from harm.

(From a postcard that Grandmother Laura sent to Grandmother Erna.)

Although we wrote faithfully from Kuma following our deportation in June of 1940, our letters failed to reach Mielec for about seven months. My grandparents had to rely on friends and relatives, in Lwów under the Soviets and even in Kraków under the Germans, for news about us. Thus, grandmother Laura often wrote to Grandmother Erna in Lwów, and Erna forwarded her cards to us. At last, on February 7, 1941, Grandmother Laura writes: 'For the first time, we have today received directly from you two cards from Leon and Andzia, which has rejoiced us a great deal, and at the same time we are sad for being so far away from one another, and for your destiny.'

Even when the Jews were 'free', as was the case of my grandparents, who were not locked in a ghetto, they could not simply show up at a post office and drop a letter into a box. 'Gusta is not writing to you because she does not have the right identity papers which permit one to be writing [to the Soviet Union],' Grandmother says about her sister in Kraków. At the same time, Gusta was receiving mail from us and forwarding it to her sister. It was a twisted world replete with sadistic touches. My grandparents were allowed to receive letters with enclosures (though postcards were less likely to get 'lost' at the censors), but they themselves could only mail open postcards, with only one single person allowed to write on any given card. Grandmother writes: 'Tato [Grandfather Leib] will write separately because we are not allowed to

101

write together.' And again: 'Tato cannot add anything, as adding something to a letter is forbidden.' Yet the two sisters played at fooling the censors, once Gusta had moved in with Laura in late 1940, and Gusta would occasionally hide one or two lines inside Grandmother's text.

'Before they left us, we asked them and begged them to stay with us, but to no avail,' Laura Blattberg wrote from Mielec to Erna Schreiber in Lwów. O, how my grandparents had begged us to stay with them in Mielec because 'no harm would come to women and children!' They were consumed by anguish about our fate. 'That which has befallen us we could still endure if only we could shield the children from harm,' wrote Grandmother Laura to Grandmother Schreiber in October. They imagined us starving and freezing to death in a gulag. And indeed, of those deported to the Soviet Union, about a quarter had died before the July 1941 clemency which set us free from Kuma.

It is hard to guess how much my grandparents really knew about the condition of deportees to the Soviet Union. It seems that during the late fall and early winter of 1939–40 some information was available on both sides of the border. Mail, of course, was censored but people still moved back and forth even after the borders were closed in late October. Incredible as it might now seem, large numbers were crossing back to the west, from the USSR to the General-gouvernement, as I have mentioned before. They were returning to share the fate of their families or, simply, to stand in solidarity with their people.

At the same time, many were still crossing in the opposite direction: Jews who were trying to escape and Jews expelled by the Germans, like the unfortunates from the Lublinland Reservation. The Soviets at first kept pushing the refugees back, but eventually, fed up with it all, they began deportations for political 're-education'. A few deportees managed to escape in the beginning and their tales may have reached as far as Mielec. There were also underground couriers, like the young man whom Mark Verstandig mentioned in his memoir and who smuggled messages between Lwów and Mielec until he himself disappeared in early 1940.

In her card to us dated October 10, 1940, Grandmother wrote that she was extremely anxious about our fate because 'it was known that people from those parts make excursions into various directions'. Substitute 'Soviet zone' for 'those parts' and 'are deported' for 'make excursions' and the cipher is broken. My grandparents' imagination was so inflamed that they convinced themselves we would have been better off staying with them in Mielec. They obviously did not yet realize what was in store for them.

Kuma's location in the middle of nowhere was exacerbating their sense of anguish and confusion. They probably asked themselves, Where is Mariyskaya ASSR, and what on earth is an ASSR? I can well imagine them poring over their old atlas of tsarist Russia, where no mention of Mariyskaya ASSR would appear, since the Autonomous Soviet Socialist Republics were newly created administrative entities. 'I simply cannot imagine how you manage there now, nor do I know in what area is this place located and what kind of a climate it has,' laments Grandmother. And later, a small triumph is celebrated: 'I knew right away that you would be in some sort of forest labor because I had talked to a man who knows that country, hoping he might inform me more or less about your location.'

The Landau women were well educated, but their frame of reference was the tsarist Russia of their youth. 'Where is this place located, in what gubernia?' Gusta asks us, using the tsarist word for 'province'. And she sounds almost relieved upon learning that her sister-in-law Binka Landau was in Archangelsk; it may have been by the Arctic Circle, but at least she knew where it was.

As for us, we were inside the giant 'V' formed by the confluence of the Volga and Kama Rivers. This is a region where peoples of Asiatic origin – Tuctic, Finno-Ugric and Tatar minorities – mix with the Russians. Our lot fell with the Finno-Ugric family, first with the Mari of Kuma and later with the Udmurt of Kambarka. The Mari were the dominant ethnic group in the Kuma area and thus were granted their own Autonomous Republic there. However, I don't think that we ourselves knew exactly where we were, and much less cared about the various Soviet administrative entities. Yet I can understand, so very well, that Grandmother Laura felt compelled to create for herself at least a visualization of our surroundings.

Like leaves in the wind we were all scattered. Grandmother Blattberg's anguish was without bounds. She despaired for us in Kuma and for her first-born son in Lithuania. She agonized over her sister in Kraków, and her brother in England, and her sister-in-law alone somewhere in the depths of Russia, and her niece in Lwów, and all the others. However, she was not one passively to await destiny. That much is clear from her cards.

In the summer of 1940 she traveled to Kraków at least twice – a difficult undertaking, but not impossible, as the Mielec Jews were not imprisoned in a ghetto. From her cards we can infer that she was both able to secure the necessary travel permits and brave enough to endure a train ride while branded with her Star of David armband.

To Grandmother Erna in Lwów she writes: 'I have recently visited my sister Gusta, also your sister Mrs Wassertheil and the Schwarzes, and I even was in your apartment on Agnieszka. They were all supposed to leave but have remained for the time being. The air in our place is rather mild and we are not feeling too badly.'

And to us in Kuma she says: ' Gusta is not writing to you because she does not have the right identity papers which permit one to be writing. They were supposed to come to us but have received an extension of their residency. I recently went to visit her.'

The Jews of Kraków were not yet walled up inside the ghetto, but their situation was both confusing and terrifying. On the one hand their numbers had swelled due to the influx of Jews expelled from rural areas; whilst on the other, they themselves were living with the daily dread of mass expulsions. This came about as the result of two contradictory edicts. The first edict was issued on September 21, 1939, when Heydrich instructed the Einsatzgruppen to concentrate the Jews expelled from small communities onto reservations or into large cities. The second came after Kraków was made the seat of the Generalgouvernement. All Jews of Kraków, except those who were deemed 'economically indispensable', were to leave 'voluntarily'. Not many 'volunteered' and the Germans eventually began mass expulsions.

Thus Grandmother Laura's mention of her visit to 'your sister Mrs Wassertheil and the Schwarzes, and even... your apartment on Agnieszka' was meant to hearten Grandmother Erna by telling her that her family, the Wassertheils and the Schwarzes, were still in their own apartments, still in Kraków, at least 'for the time being'.

'Gusta is still in Kraków for the time being, her things are here, who knows how things will be,' writes Laura again on October 7. Gusta herself also writes: 'I still live at the same address but, because another landlady wants to take over this apartment, I don't know how it will be. I have managed to get identity papers.'

Grandmother's reference to the relative mildness of 'the air in our place' is a comment not about weather, as we learn from Gusta that frost had in fact set in very early that year, but rather about the relative lull in persecution within Mielec at the time of her writing. It was a time when Hitler, Himmler, and Heydrich were still experimenting with approaches to the 'final solution', and the killing machine was still sputtering here or there. Perhaps it is partly for that reason that my grandparents still thought we should have stayed with them in Mielec.

Like leaves in the wind we were all scattered. While we were running for Lwów, Papa's brother Wilek, his wife Mania and my cousin Gila, who was my senior by more than ten years, ran for Wilno, a city that had been part of Poland during the interwar years. However, on September 28, 1939, as they were signing the German–Soviet Boundary and Friendship Treaty for the partition of Poland, the Russians also concluded pacts with the three Baltic countries. They 'gave' Polish Wilno* to Lithuania in exchange for rights to military bases, and Uncle Wilek suddenly found himself living in an independent country. This independence was, however, short-lived. The USSR annexed and occupied the three Baltic states less than a

---

*Now Vilnius, capital of Lithuania.

year later. At the time of Grandmother's writing, Uncle Wilek, once again a Polish refugee in the Soviet Union, and therefore a potential 'spy', was living with the threat of deportation to the depths of Russia. An intellectual and a published author, he was especially vulnerable.

Wilek and Mania, however, had another plan. Mania's brother, who lived in the United States, had sent them an 'Affidavit', the magic piece of paper that enabled one to apply for an immigration visa to the United States under the minuscule Jewish quota allowed by the State Department. Of course, they also needed a transit visa that would permit them to cross the Soviet Union into Japan, and from there to the United States.

We learn all this from Grandmother's cards: 'Wilek writes fairly often saying that his brother-in-law is trying to arrange for them passage to America, but there are difficulties. I would be glad if this were to happen. I cannot enclose Wilek's letters.'

And again: 'Wilek is in Wilno. He writes that he does not have steady work, but he manages.'

There are allusions to their travails in Grandmother's cards. 'We have not had any news from Wilek lately, but that's his way, although he has been much improved lately. It's not possible to send him packages either. It is also very difficult for him to realize his project of leaving for A. [to get a visa to the United States] because he does not have a steady job there,' she writes us on December 30. Two days later she adds: 'Wilek wrote saying that Mania is again in Kovno [i.e. Kaunas, then capital of Lithuania] regarding their departure to A. He writes that it may be possible to arrange.' At last, in March of 1941, Laura writes: 'Like I already wrote you, we have recently had news from Wilek from Moscow that he is going to ride by express train to Japan. May God grant they arrive safely to their destination.' This is followed by: 'We have received today a letter from Wilek from Japan. He is very satisfied with his trip.'

Uncle Wilek's itinerary – from Kovno to Moscow to Vladivostok to Tokyo – was followed by the many Jews whose lives were saved by the Japanese consul in Kovno, Chiune Sugihara, who issued for them transit visas through Japan, in defiance of explicit orders from the Foreign Ministry in Tokyo.

The Soviet Union had already annexed Lithuania, and the consulate would close on August 28, 1940, but Sugihara kept writing transit visa forms until the very last moment, putting in a fake final destination to what was then the Dutch East Indies. While the British, American, and French consuls, on instruction from their governments, refused to issue transit visas to Jewish refugees, Sugihara decided to disobey his superiors, and he saved thousands of Jews at the expense of his own career.

Wilek, Mania, and Gila eventually reached New York, traveling from Tokyo to Honolulu and then to San Francisco. We did not hear from them until the spring of 1945, when we were about to starve in Kambarka. Suddenly one day, like manna from Heaven, five packages arrived all sewn inside hempcloth, and we did not starve. (But I have written about this already...)

Like leaves in the wind we were all scattered. Grand-uncle Szymek Landau, Grandmother Laura's brother, was in England on a business trip when the war broke out. His wife Binka fled to Lwów in order to take refuge with her two brothers, the Beck family who were so helpful to us when we staggered into Lwów in the autumn of 1939. Binka was a pampered prewar lady who had never worked outside of her home and who did not know how to earn a living. Thus, a 'useless bourgeois capitalist', she was deported to Archangelsk under very harsh conditions. She was completely cut off from the family for about six months. Laura and Gusta were sick with worry about their sister-in-law, who was all alone and ill-prepared to fend for herself. 'We have absolutely no news from Szymek, and I don't know Binka's whereabouts,' Grandmother writes.

'We have absolutely no news of Binka and Szymek. I am especially worried about Binka because I fear for her health. Her separation from Szymek was already such a tragic blow and now I don't even know where she is,' Gusta writes in November. And a few days later, she adds, 'I have indirect news from Szymek, he is looking for Binka. I accidentally happened to learn that she is in Archangelsk, but I don't have her address.'

Gusta could not have received *direct* news from her brother in England when England and Germany were at war. I am speculating, without a shred of evidence, that her conduit for '*indirect news*' may have been one of the two mysterious characters in neutral Switzerland whom Grandmother mentions in February of 1941: '... they wrote me from the Red Cross in Switzerland that it is possible to send parcels from a neutral country, and maybe Uncle Moses could and this is why I had the idea of writing to Mettler.' I don't know if we received any parcels from Uncle Moses or Mr Mettler, and I have never heard about either of them, but it was still possible for a Jew from the Generalgouvernement to correspond with people in Switzerland.

At the same time, it should have been possible to establish direct communication between England and the Soviet Union, but suspicion of anything 'Western' was such that an exchange of letters was just too overwhelming for the censors. Who knows what sinister plot might be hatching between the lines of a letter? A telegram was as much as they could bear. 'We had news from Binka this week,' says Grandmother in March of 1941. 'She writes that her only contact with Szymek is by telegram, that Andzia has sent her some things for the winter.' And elsewhere she writes: 'Mrs Schreiber wrote that you are sending Binka packages. We have received one post-card from Binka but have absolutely no news from Szymek.'

Mama was one of the most giving people that I have ever met. She must have decided that Binka, all alone by the Arctic Circle, needed warm clothes even more than she did. She would often tell me, 'You will never regret what you did for other people, but you will always regret what you have *not* done for them.' This was Mama's own version of Hillel's precept, 'If you are for yourself alone, who are you?' (Unfortunately, she seems to have forgotten the first half of that injunction, 'If you are not for yourself, who will be?')

The family member best able to send parcels to Binka was her husband's niece, and Papa's cousin, Hela Landau – whom Grandmother Laura often calls 'our Helusia', in order to distinguish her from the other Helas in the family. A talented pianist, 'our Helusia' had a successful career in Lwów. We know about her performances from a Soviet newspaper clipping and also from a card that Grandmother Schreiber sent us from Lwów in May of 1940. 'Hela earns very well, she has constantly concert performances, one also hears her on the radio, a capable woman,' writes Grandmother Erna. The reference to Hela's excellent salary is a reminder of the value that the Soviets placed on talented performers, who were considered a national treasure.

Following an initial mention of a letter in September 1940, both Laura and Gusta repeatedly complain that they have 'no news of Helusia'. All I know is that 'our Helusia' sent us at least one package to Kuma, and I know this from Grandmother Schreiber's tip to Mama about getting rid of the smell of naphthalene mothballs in sugar: 'Anduś, maybe you can air the sugar you received from Hela, maybe this will draw out some of the naphthalene; the fabric was [packed] in naphthalene.'

Hela Landau was killed by the Germans, so I have no memory of her. I imagine her as a gentle, absent-minded intellectual like her brother Tulek, who survived because he had been studying in England when the war broke out. Who but a dreamy artist would inform Grandmother Laura that we were safe and forget to include our address, or pack mothballs and sugar in the same container?

Binka was released from her camp after the Stalin–Sikorski 'amnesty' agreement of July 1941, and she spent the rest of the war in Central Asia. We were already back from Kambarka when Binka was repatriated in mid-1946, and she lived with us for several months while awaiting her exit papers for England. We were trying to fatten her up so Uncle Szymek would not 'mistake her for a scarecrow' upon her arrival in London. She ate and ate, and one could almost see her filling out in slow motion. 'I have to stop eating before I get too fat for the plane to take off with me inside it,' she would joke. The planes were patched-up tin boxes with motors that sounded as if they were about to draw their last breath. However, Binka did take off safely and was reunited with Uncle Szymek and their nephew Tulek. They all later moved to Tel Aviv. Both of Tulek's sons are artists – one of them a concert pianist.

Grandmother Laura devoted a good chunk of her considerable energy and her meager resources to give shape to her twin obsessions: arranging for delivery of packages to us in Kuma, while at the same time trying to bring us back from there.

Sending us parcels of food and clothing became her mission. 'As far as packages are concerned, we'll do everything we can because we feel inside ourselves compelled to do it,' she writes.

For the first seven months, they were forbidden to send anything directly from Mielec. 'We cannot send anything from here,' Laura writes on a number of occasions. The first mention of a package sent from Mielec appears in February of 1941. Meanwhile, she was begging friends and relatives in Lwów to send us packages: 'We are extremely glad that... [Neuhof] is sending you some food that you need. I have already written to a number of people asking them to send you packages but I don't know if anyone has done anything.' Her anxiety was compounded by the erratic mail delivery. She never knew who had responded and who hadn't; who had or had not been able to send a package to us. And, bearing in mind that everyone was dirt poor, how was one to reimburse them? One couldn't send money orders. Grandmother used all sorts of approaches: 'I will give the money here to his wife who is in Tarnów' or 'I'll pay his mother here,' she writes.

The packages that we received from our family in Lwów and in Mielec were vital to us; in the literal sense of the word 'vital', they enabled us to survive. Duduś puts it this way: 'Our parents have saved our lives by sending us packages from Tarnów to Kuma. Not so much in Kuma but later, when we were starving in Kazakhstan. For two full years we were able to barter the clothing from our parents' packages for food – a pair of slacks here, a shirt there. We would not have survived otherwise.'

For the Wassertheils and ourselves, who did not have the Schiff brothers' *Stakahanovist* rations, with two growing children to feed, with Uncle Jules a semi-invalid, and Papa 'not much of a worker', the bartering and selling started quite early. 'I am saddened to hear that Leon had to sell his suits. I have mailed you two whole suits and walking shoes and will send more,' Grandmother writes in her very last postcard.

No doubt the suits that Papa was forced to sell were taken

apart at the seams and recut, because, long-armed and long-legged, he was much taller than the local Maris. Papa must have been quite a sight in that wilderness with his prewar suits tailored from the finest English wool and his hand-made city shoes that had never seen any mud. 'Dear Andzia, you write about galoshes for Leon. I have inquired everywhere, there aren't any. I'll try again,' Grandmother writes. And again later: 'I have written Schiff concerning the galoshes for you but have not received an answer either.'

Papa always had problems with shoes; he had flat feet, and they were big – size 13 – which may not seem much nowadays, but was enormous at that time. It did not matter in his youth, as it was customary then to have shoes hand-made by a cobbler, but during the war it became a major problem. Papa had no shoes! Duduś, who had inherited big feet from his mother's, the Schwarz side of the family (who were nicknamed the 'long soles from Chrzanów'), was in a similar predicament. This is why Grandmother, hoping they might have some huge galoshes to spare, wrote to the elder Schiffs in Tarnów.

For the remainder of the war, Papa walked in *lapcies* stuffed with rags and newspapers. Mama and I had feet of normal size and we had the traditional Russian *valenki*, a pull-on boot made of thick felt, to keep us reasonably warm. But we had another problem; my feet refused to stop growing and I constantly needed new shoes. However, back in Kuma, the problem of footwear was mainly Papa's, and this topic keeps recurring in Grandmother's cards: 'I can imagine how difficult it is there for Leon as far as shoes, what with his sensitive feet that were always difficult to fit,' – or 'Leon, how are your legs, do you have any bandages?'

Almost every card from Mielec and from Lwów is about packages; how to send them, what to send, what has arrived, what has been lost, what has been returned. It makes for tedious reading, but these postcards are not about literature. They are about love. It is a poignant irony that those who were about to die, the Blattbergs of Mielec and the Schiffs of Tarnów, gave their children a parting gift of life.

Bringing us back, from Kuma to Lwów, became another obsession for Laura, although, try as I might, I cannot imagine how one could have hoped to accomplish this. She was moving heaven and earth: 'We think about you constantly and are trying to arrange that you may be where Andzia's Mama is [i.e., back in Lwów]'.

'We are going to do everything we can to change your place of stay,' she writes in November. The same message recurs, again and again. She even writes openly, 'We are all trying to arrange for your return to Lwów.' Poor Grandmother was tortured by her failure to 'change our place of stay'.

Dear Babuniu Blattbereczek, wherever you may be now, please rest assured that you did not fail. It is crystal clear that the Russians, by taking us to Kuma, saved our lives. Given my father's nature – 'And you, Leon, with your sensitivity to everything!' – there is not one chance in a million that we would have survived under the Germans, on Aryan papers or in any other way.

About her own situation, Grandmother tells us nothing. A few words slip by here or there to reveal her misery. 'So far we have received nothing from Gliny but hope to get some staples,' she writes in October, already over thirteen months into the war. And she adds: 'Gusta is still in Kraków for the time being, her things are here, who knows how things will be.'

The estate at Gliny Wielkie, which used to sustain the Blattberg family, had been expropriated in the fall of 1939. It was placed in the hands of a *Treuhandler* (a Volksdeutsch* trustee), who had complete discretion concerning the amount of produce that he would or would not give to my grandparents. As of October 1940, it appears that he had not given them anything. In a subsequent postcard Grandmother writes, 'We have received something from Gliny,' but without specifying what that 'something' was.

My grandparents never complained. 'Do not worry about us; we have everything we need,' they always wrote. It was almost like a litany. Perhaps they had resources other than from Gliny. In the beginning, they most probably had some gold, silver and jewelry, the standard accoutrements of prewar bourgeois life, but I don't know if anything was left after the German confiscation decrees and the 'payments' which the

---

*Ethnic German living in Poland before the war.

Judenrat administration was often forced to deliver in order to ransom Jewish hostages.

All in all, I know very little about the material conditions of my grandparents' life. I do not think that they were hungry during the period of our correspondence, but perhaps I am wrong. From a card that Gusta wrote in November of 1940, we know that 'Winter has started early. Already in September it was cold and in October potatoes have frozen in some areas. Fortunately, the harvest for this item was so huge that people are buying it not only by the cubic meter but by the cart-load, and even by the wagon-load. It's also relatively inexpensive.' Thus, potatoes at least appear to have been in abundant supply at that point.

No doubt barter played a great role. Our own clothes from before the war may have provided another source of supply. Grandmother mentions that her sister Gusta's 'things are here,' and that suggests that she or Gusta herself was able to transport them from Kraków. Grandmother later writes that she was able to mail some of Papa's clothes, but not some others that he had requested, because she did 'not have access to them'. She similarly writes that she was not able to get hold of Mama's ski-suit. Does this mean that she was able to remove some clothes from our apartment at the very beginning of the war? It would appear so: in May of 1941 she writes, 'I am sending Leon's shoes that came from Krasinskiego,' referring to our prewar apartment on Aleja Krasinskiego. And again: 'Leon, you mention your trench-coat with the lining, but unfortunately I have not received it from Krasinskiego but I do have other things which I want to send you, and I do send things often.'

Dr and Mrs Nowak, our next door Polish neighbors on Aleja Krasinskiego, probably had a key to the apartment. All I know for certain is that in October or November of 1939 our apartment was taken over by an official of the General-gouvernement who greatly enjoyed the fruits of Mama's labor. Mrs Nowak told us after the war that the German official was most impressed by Mama's pantry and its shelves laden with jars of home-made jams and preserves. 'A most excellent *Hausfrau* used to live here,' he exclaimed.

10 *The Price of Eggs*

And now Andzia, do not torture this sweet little bird so much with recitations of poems, she is too little, at least leave her alone in the summer.

(From one of Grandmother Erna's postcards.)

As one reads the postcards from Mielec, several stories unfold between September of 1940 and May of 1941. Uncle Wilek is in Wilno [Vilnius] and he is trying for months to get a visa to the United States. At last he is in Moscow, then in Tokyo. Great-aunt Gusta is in Kraków, she is expelled from Kraków and she moves in with my grandparents. Other characters appear, as a watermark on a sheet of stationery. Yet during all that time we learn absolutely nothing about my grandparents, who repeat incessantly 'do not worry about us, we have our health and we have what we need'. There is but one unguarded moment as Grandmother Laura writes in German to Grandmother Erna: 'That which has befallen us we could still endure if only we could shield the children from harm.'

There is a mask over the Mielec cards. Only the punctuation, the complete absence of it in the original text, hints at Grandmother Laura's anguish. It is not just that we don't learn anything about my grandparents' fate; what is more remarkable still is that not one relative or friend in Mielec is mentioned. Who is still allowed to work, who is still in town, who is in a forced-labor gang and who is in the slave-labor camp at Pustków? We learn nothing. The giant shadow of the German censor blots out everything.

The postcards from Lwów are completely different. There are only five remaining, all of them written at the end of May 1941, and their tone is almost chatty. 'I wrote yesterday,' Grandmother Erna tells us, 'yet I feel like writing again today, maybe it's a conversation with you, Andeczka, from so far away.'

The Soviet cards do not look menacing. In contrast to the swastika and the German eagle, the hammer-and-sickle emblem and the Soviet stamp that depicts a young girl with a kerchief on her head appear quite cheerful. When Uncle Menek writes his name on the return address in the Russian way, Menachem Abramovitch [Menachem son of Abraham] this too is somehow reassuring. Of course, the censors read everything, but the mail goes directly to Kuma without detouring at 'central processing' in Moscow, and although delivery is erratic it is only a matter of dealing with the vagaries of the internal postal system.

There is no mask of stoicism. Human foibles, self-pity, whining, anger and jealousy are readily apparent. The cast of characters is pretty much the same as before: there is Uncle Menek's wife Hela – and Hela Landau, Papa's cousin, who is a pianist; there is Guscia Schiff in Tarnów – and Guscia Maj, the mother of my playmate Henryś [Heneczek]; there is Basia Beck, my former babysitter from Lwów, who was extremely devoted to us. There are 'the boys', the three Schiff brothers, in Kuma. Many other friends and relatives appear as well. Several names are abbreviated so that I don't really know who Grandmother is talking about, but in her own incoherent, rambling way she portrays a slice of refugee life in Lwów a few weeks before the German invasion. A housewife with only a grammar school education, Grandmother carries out her 'conversation' with us by talking about things that define her everyday life – her son's wages, the price of milk, the price of eggs, the availability of chicken. We learn a great deal in this way.

We learn that even at this late hour, people still live in fear of deportation, daintily named 'excursions to your parts'.

'One lives in constant nervous tension,' Grandmother writes, 'always thinking about an excursion to your parts. Several have left already, like Binka's brothers.' Their Soviet citizenship notwithstanding, Uncle Menek, his wife and Grandmother could easily have been deported for any manner of anti-Soviet offense real or imaginary.

We learn that in the Soviet Union money does matter, it matters very much, and we learn how much of it is needed to survive.

'The mother-in-law of Guscia Maj told me that her nephew Silbiger lives with them. He contributes to their support, he earns 400 rubles, she still must add 100r. herself to survive.' Womenfolk in those days were forever dependent and expected their men to support them. 'What's going to happen when the boy goes off to military service? This is how things are nowadays,' laments Grandmother.

Poor Uncle Menek was constantly pressured from all sides. He was working very hard. Grandmother writes: 'Menek... earns 320r., he also works overtime, he earns altogether maybe 450 r[ubles].' Menek provided for his mother and his wife, who was ailing. He was constantly sending money and goods not only to his sisters Herminka, Janka and Andzia but also to his wife's family, the Oppenheims, who were 'in deportation' too.

Uncle Menek was overburdened. 'I have received your postcards,' he wrote to us.

Unfortunately, I cannot for the time being send you these packages because, as I told you already, I have no money. You well know that what I had is long gone for packages for all of you and the Oppenheims, again cash for Herminka, Hela's illnesses, and I myself have been somewhat unwell, and the rest went for food. One earns very little, it's difficult to subsist, and it's practically impossible to sell what things we have.

Menek adds: 'I cannot take from Mama anything for these parcels because after all she has nothing more left to sell. If I manage to sell something I'll immediately mail you the two packages you requested with the shoes.'

The demands on Uncle Menek never ceased. One of the Schwarz grand-uncles was making a request: 'As for Uncle Schw...,' writes Grandmother, 'I saw and read those cards, I asked Menek to take care of it right away [I told him] I would give for all this 200 r[ubles] or more. He said it's none of my business, the cards are addressed to him. I can't talk about it anymore because he gets mad; this is how things are, I'll see what comes next.'

I remember Uncle Menek very well from the postwar

period. He had a big heart, and an even bigger temper. I can well picture him shouting at Grandmother to 'mind her own business'.

But Erna knew her son. 'I'll see what comes next,' she wrote.

She was also selling off all her possessions to send us money. On May 25, she writes: 'I sent you, Andzia, money a long time ago in a newspaper. I also gave some to Basia that she should send it to you; also two books by registered mail.'

A few days later she writes again: 'I assume that you have already received the money because I put it inside the newspaper. I also gave Basia money to send to you, maybe it will reach you.'

She was sending Aunt Herminka about 500 rubles every month, more money than Uncle Menek was earning even while working overtime. I hope that he had worked out an effective way of transferring it to her, since sending money orders was akin to throwing dice. And, of course, there were no banks. As for ourselves in Kuma, I would be willing to bet that we have never received the money that Grandmother sent us 'inside the newspaper'. No doubt it stuck to the fingers of a censor or a postal clerk, but sending us the money made Grandmother feel better. The irony of it all was that she was simultaneously able to send us books by registered mail.

Grandmother was especially anguished about Aunt Herminka: 'I am not a good mother that I have allowed my husbandless child to be taken to Siberia,' she moans, as if she could have single-handedly stopped the NKVD deportations. Alone with my cousins, Marcel and Anita, Aunt Herminka was in a most difficult situation. Grandmother writes that an egg cost Herminka three rubles, and a glass of milk two rubles. 'She buys [them] for Anita and Marcel is jealous, but she cannot afford such expenses [for both children].' Were Herminka to buy one egg and one glass of milk for each child every day to supplement their rations of clay-like bread and watery broth, she would need to part with 300 of her 500 rubles – assuming, of course, that she had indeed received this amount.

Grandmother quotes the price of eggs and milk that prevailed in peacetime, shortly before the German invasion. A month or two later, the price of food had skyrocketed to the point that a single egg might cost as much as a month's wages, or more.

Grandmother was quite prone to melodramatic laments. Like the Jewish mother of lore, she was convinced that her children could not survive without her constant ministrations. Referring to a quarrel between Mama and Aunt Janka about some medicine, she writes:

> After all, you are good sisters, with a good heart to one another, the more so as you are in such an exile, orphans without father or mother, you should stick together, not to mention what is going on now when people are dying everyday; I only ask you to think about me that is left all alone, grieving over Papa, but I envy him that he doesn't see what I have lived to see, the children and grandchildren without me, your mother.

Grandmother was indulging in self-pity and, like most in her generation, she thought of herself as an old woman at the age of 60. At the same time, her postcards are strangely comforting as she gathers us all to her generous bosom. She calls Papa her 'dear Leosiu' as if he were still four years old; she scolds Mama for forcing me to recite too much poetry: 'And now Andzia, do not torture this sweet little bird so much with recitations of poems, she is too little, at least leave her alone in the summer; in Lwów already the little child had to recite verse by heart.'

Mama was making me learn by heart all of Julian Tuwim's poems for children, as well as every nursery rhyme she could think of. She was pushing me relentlessly yet, by teaching me to read and write at a very early age, she also gave me a priceless treasure, the key to my own private world, where I could dwell at will when outside things were tough.

In our household, books were as important as food. 'I have sent two books, they are not so nice. I heard that one can exchange books at your place,' Grandmother writes, referring to the book-swapping system that was put in place by the inmates at Kuma. Later, in Kambarka, it was much more difficult to find books, although there again my parents engaged in an elaborate system of borrowing and swapping. I usually had a book or two. When everything else failed, I would read from the scraps of newspapers that we cut up for use as toilet paper. It's not that I understood the text, it was the magic of the individual printed word or phrase that I prized.

The quality of the paper in Soviet books was dismal. 'They are not so nice,' Grandmother tells us with uncharacteristic understatement. Imagine my delight one day in Kambarka, when I was about seven-years-old and Papa borrowed from someone a wonderful illustrated edition of *Hamlet*. A very large book from the tsarist era, a folio with a dark-brown binding and embossed lettering that had been flattened by time, it had magnificent black and white engravings. I was enthralled by those pictures and I still carry in my eyes the image of the ghost of Hamlet's father, an immobile, huge, awe-inspiring presence. I did not find it at all strange that one would talk to the dead; after all, I myself was talking every evening to my dead grandfather. As I have already mentioned, I prayed to Dziadziusio Schreiber, asking him to shield us all from harm, to crush Hitler and to bring us safely home to Kraków.

It may well be that praying to Dziadziusio Schreiber was of some help, for Grandmother Schreiber, as well as all her children and grandchildren, came safely home to Kraków in 1945 and 1946.

Two postcards remain from that postwar period, both written by Grandmother Schreiber. In contrast to her somewhat self-pitying and melodramatic tone in 1941, the woman who writes in the fall of 1945, and who had seen the unspeakable, tells of their survival story only that 'It was a hard nut to crack but we are alive thank God, it is difficult for me to write about it.'

In their quiet, understated way, the two 1945 postcards recount the destruction of Polish Jewry. 'There are no children,' Grandmother tells us, and she speaks of the many who 'are not here' and the few, the very few, who are still 'here'. She makes a reference to the Schiff brothers, Zelek, Kalmek, and Duduś, who were still in Central Asia. When Grandmother wrote her postcard in October of 1945, the

brothers already knew that their parents were dead –
deported on the first transport from Tarnów to the death camp
of Belzec – but they still clung to the hope that their sister
Gusta, and Zelek's young wife Hanka were alive. An
eyewitness had seen the two young women alive in Kraków
just a few weeks before the city's liberation in January of 1945.
They were still living there on Aryan papers when the
Russians were already at the gates of the city. When
Grandmother, Aunt Hela and Uncle Menek returned to
Kraków in April of 1945, Gusta and Hanka were gone. In
October, Grandmother writes to us: 'Zelek Schiff... called, the
poor man is looking for Hanka and Gusta, may God grant
they still emerge from some camp.'

'When we came back in 1946,' Duduś later told us, 'we
thought we had something to come back to.' Alas, it was not
meant to be. The brothers learned that Hanka and Gusta had
died in Auschwitz, denounced at the last minute by a Jew who
had been caught by the Gestapo. Brought up in an Orthodox
household, each brother reacted to his loss in his own
individual way; thus Zelek completely stopped praying while
Duduś still puts on his *tefilim* and his *tales* every single day of
his life and prays in memory of his parents and his sister.

11   My Poland

The word 'depression' was never used but, looking back at 1946 with hindsight, I can see that Mama went through a period of depression following our return from Kambarka and her recovery from pneumonia. We were already living in an apartment on Aleja Słowackiego and Mama was keeping house after a fashion, but she was listless, indifferent, she had no appetite and she stayed in bed for a good part of the day.

I spent a lot of time at Grandmother's or at Aunt Janka's, where I played with my cousin Romeczek and our friend Henryś Maj. And for the first time in my life, I had girl friends of about my age, mostly Jewish girls who had survived in Russia but also several Polish girls whose parents had not raised them for blind hatred.

I even had a Russian friend, Ludmilla, who lived in our apartment building. She wore a red bow in her hair and amazing red underpants of rough cotton that her mother had cut from a Soviet flag. Ludmilla and her brother spoke passable Polish but neither her mother nor her father understood a word of it. This was rather amusing as her father, who always wore an impeccable Polish uniform, was a colonel in the Polish army. He was one of a group of Russian officers whom the Soviet overlords of postwar Poland had instantly promoted to Polish citizenship simply because they could lay claim to some distant Polish ancestry. Thus a ready-made nucleus of loyal communist cadres was inserted into Polish society.

It was difficult for me to cope with Mama's protracted illness. Moreover, I was excruciatingly shy and awkward. An innocent who gave her heart away much too quickly, I had a rather painful apprenticeship, yet every day brought its share of wonderment and discovery. I learned to play hopscotch, to skip, to ride a bike, to push elevator buttons and turn the knobs on a tunable radio. There were incredible things to eat: chicken, butter, jams, even chocolate. There were such things as stores where one could actually buy things. About once a week, Grandmother gave me five zlotys, enough for a small portion of a heavenly ice-cream that was cleverly sandwiched between two flat rectangular wafers.

I got a library card from a lending library close to Grandmother's house and spent wondrous hours on benches in the Planty park reading the classics of Polish literature with a passion so intense that I cannot even find the words to express it. We were already living in our apartment on Aleja Słowackiego but I often visited Grandmother for lunch, so that it was very easy for me to run over to the library for my precious ration of books. Alas, they were doled out one volume at a time. When I saw that Sienkiewiczes' fantastic saga *Ogniem i Mieczem* [By the Fire and by the Sword] consisted of two volumes, I decided to read the first one in the park and then fetch the second one on my way home. The story in the first volume was so fascinating that I went on reading the second volume under my shady tree, instead of going home. Besides, I had no watch to remind me of the passing hours and home was incredibly depressing, as Mama was still very weak and pretty much bedridden.

I can't remember if my reading of *Ogniem i Mieczem* took place before or after the Kielce pogrom of July 4, 1946, but it must have been close to that date because it was 1946 and the sun set very late. Needless to say, my parents were beside themselves with panic when I failed to show up at home. As we did not have a phone, Papa ran to Grandmother's only to be told that I had been gone for hours. Uncle Menek advised against going to the police, saying that they might do more harm than good (it seems that after the August 1945 pogrom in Kraków, policemen assigned to protecting the wounded in the hospital had attacked them instead).

Friends and relatives were enlisted into a frantic search of the town. They went to Aunt Janka's house, to the house of my best friend Irka Fenichel, they scoured every nook and cranny until at last someone found me around 9 p.m. still sitting on my bench in the gathering dusk and contentedly reading the last few chapters of the second volume. The reception that awaited me at home was such that I became a model of punctuality for the rest of my life.

All in all, I was a reliable child and there were few breaches of discipline. One that I still remember involved Great-aunt Binka and that heavenly ice-cream so cleverly sandwiched between two flat wafers. Great-aunt Binka, Great-uncle Szymek Landau's wife, was living with us upon her return from Russia, like many others who stayed in our apartment for a few weeks or a few months before moving on. Aunt Binka was waiting to be reunited with Szymek, who had spent the war in England, and she had some money that he had sent her from there. One afternoon she gave me five zlotys for ice-cream. However, she handed it to me as a ten-zloty bill because she had no change. 'Mind you,' she admonished me, 'don't forget to bring me back the change.' That was easier said than done as, for the first time in my life, I was actually holding in my hand enough money to buy the large ten-zloty sandwich, a thick slab of ice-cream so much more satisfying than the puny little five-zloty size. I had been lusting for it for months already and, of course, I bought it.

Although she had helped raise Tulek and Hela Landau following their parents' fatal car crash, Aunt Binka had no children of her own and she was something of a martinet. She immediately went to tell Mama about my unauthorized purchase of the ten-zloty ice-cream. I had to endure a humiliating, lengthy sermon about 'reliability' and 'trustworthiness' and 'honoring one's word'. Right then and there I resolved that when I would grow up I would not stay home like Mama, but instead go to work and earn my own living and not have to beg anyone for ice-cream money. And so I did.

My parents held me to very high standards. War or no war, displacement or no displacement, they expected me to conform to their Victorian ideal of a well-behaved child. It was essentially impossible to please them, no matter how hard I tried, but, far from being a crushing burden, the weight of their expectations helped to ground me in the midst of our unsteady lives. It gave me a frame of reference no matter what our circumstances. Brutally uprooted at the age of two, and again at three, and then again at four, and at nine, and at eleven, I was always steadied by this discipline. I knew that my parents expected me to behave and to study hard as if nothing had happened, and therefore I tried to rise to their expectations.

But a price must be paid for everything. I paid with terrifying nightmares. Volodya's little black devils from Kambarka were long since gone, but in their place came two far more sinister apparitions, both of them spawned by my fear of Polish violence. No one told me anything about violence directly because the grown-ups behaved according to the doctrine of '*obronić dziecko*' [to shield the child], which demanded they keep silent about bad things, but I knew a great deal just the same.

It was not difficult. Our apartment was like a boarding house for friends and relatives and I had a keen sense of hearing. I knew that Papa had barely escaped with his life when he went back to Mielec, I knew about the Kielce pogrom and about Jews being murdered inside trains. I can't remember whether I had already heard that during the war the Poles of Tymbark had butchered every single Jew in town – and then claimed the Germans did it – except for one boy who hid in the woods and lived to tell the story. And of course, I had my own experiences.

I believe that I have already mentioned my visions of a vengeful Christ who called for retribution against me, the Christ-killer. Even more terrifying was a night visitor who came under the guise of an innocuous old woman. In this particular nightmare, we were living in the apartment on Aleja Słowackiego and my parents were taking an afternoon nap. When the doorbell rang, I opened the door and led into the entrance hall a stooped old woman who was leaning on a cane. She was covered with a black cloak and her head was wrapped in a black kerchief. She whispered in a feeble voice, 'I am a cleaning lady and have come to help your mother with the housechores until she recovers.' Before I had the chance to wonder how this weak old woman would manage any housework, the visitor shed her concealing garments and her stooping posture. A strong, tall woman stood in front of me. Her cane became a sharp butcher knife as she strode confidently in the direction of my parents' bedroom. I knew with excruciating certitude that she was going to kill them in their sleep; I tried to scream, but I had no voice. I stood mute and frozen to the floor in utter helplessness. Merciful terror always woke me up before the murder took place, with my heart pounding out of control.

Great-aunt Binka was sleeping in my room during that period, but she was a heavy sleeper who seldom woke up. Besides, Aunt Binka was the last person I would have chosen for a confidante. And my nightmares were my own business; it would have been unseemly to bother the adults with my problems.

The nightmares grew worse after Grandmother died at the beginning of December 1946. She had accepted me unconditionally, without any expectations. She called me her '*ptaszyna*' [sweet little bird] and she delighted in my presence. It was enough for her that I had returned and was there, and now she was gone forever.

Mama took to her bed again after Grandmother's funeral. This is how I found out that Grandmother was dead. Nobody had told me anything – again the 'shield the child' principle – as if they could have concealed the death for more than a few days. By keeping it a secret they only succeeded in piling guilt on top of my heartbreak. I felt guilty for being at school when Grandmother died and for playing with my friends when she was already growing cold in her grave.

Mama roused herself from her bed in time for my tenth birthday on January 11, 1947. Though it would have been an utterly insignificant celebration by today's standards, my birthday then was a big shindig. Some ten children were assembled around the table. We ate cake and everybody sang, '*Sto lat, sto lat, niech żyje, żyje nam!*' [May she live a hundred years!], the Polish way of singing 'Happy Birthday'. Yet, although I felt grateful for all of Mama's baking and preparations, I also felt very sad because we were in mourning for Grandmother, whom I missed terribly.

I still have a scrapbook that I received on the occasion of that birthday. The size of a large wallet, it is bound in wood and carved with the picture of a church surrounded by four red and green flowers. The two wood covers are held together by a green string with an ornamental tassel. My birthday guests wrote greetings, jokes, 'secrets', poems, which they decorated with colorful drawings. My friend Ludmilla wrote a few lines in Russian.

Every girl in those days had similar scrapbooks. They were called *pamiętniki*, books of souvenirs. The *pamiętnik* from my tenth birthday has additional entries from Polish girls in my class, drawings and little notes contributed by them during the course of 1947. For 1948 – or rather for January and February of 1948, since we left Kraków in March of that year – I have another *pamiętnik*, carved with the head of a *góral*, a mountaineer from the Tatry, and some mountain flowers. The entries are signed with names such as Nowak Maria, Koziol Zofia, K. Zielinska, Palczynska Zosia – names of Polish girls bold enough to associate with a little Jewess, despite intense peer pressure to the contrary. None came to my rescue when I was attacked by a bunch of older kids, but I did not expect them to do it. They had done enough for me just by treating me like a normal human being.

On the surface, my Jewish friends and I behaved like the Polish ten-year-olds – the same fits of giggling, the same *pamiętniki*, the same ignorance about 'the facts of life'. About the latter, we were incredibly naive. One of my friends was convinced that in order to make a baby the mother and the father must lie down motionless side-by-side for hours, with the father's head at the mother's feet, and vice-versa. 'If that's the case, they better not have smelly feet,' another girl added and we all broke down in a fit of embarrassed giggling.

Just below the surface, however, ran a chasm between ourselves and the Polish girls that went much deeper than the issue of religion. It was as if, along with their baptismal certificates, the Polish girls had received the gift of something priceless that would elude us forever – the right to be who they were and where they were and a feeling of entitlement to life, of rootedness that we could only dream of. The Polish girls were chatting merrily about their First Communion gowns, about Aunt Zosia's pilgrimage to the shrine of Częstochowa, or the mouthwatering sausage that Uncle Staszek had brought from the farm. We had nothing to say. Even the air we breathed was borrowed from the Polish girls.

Our apartment on Aleja Słowackiego was always filled with friends and relatives on their way out of Poland. They began to leave in early 1947. I had to steel myself to be a bit more parsimonious in the giving of my affection, for every time someone left there was pain. Aunt Herminka, Marcel and Anita were the first to leave, to be reunited with Uncle Lonek in Buenos Aires. Aunt Janka and Uncle Jules followed them there with my beloved cousin Romeczek, whom I never saw again, as he died of leukemia. Uncle Menek, Aunt Hela and little Adaś left for Paris. Great-aunt Binka left for England. Great-aunt Sarah, who also lived with us for some time, and whom I grew to love dearly, left for a displaced persons camp in Germany. Some of my playmates left as well but, fortunately, my best friend Irka stayed for as long as we did.

The Schiff brothers lived with us for several months while waiting to leave for Palestine. A number of people were being smuggled there by the Bricha, an underground movement that had couriers and relays in Italy, France and Cyprus. As a leader of the Bricha, Duduś was often away in Łódz and Warsaw, but when he was home it was a feast for me, as I loved his buoyant personality and his strong baritone voice. I saw little of Zelek. On the other hand, Kalmek, the middle brother, was often home. A quiet man with a curly shock of hair, he was missing a finger on his left hand as a result of a work accident in Russia. He was an observant Jew who always put on his *tefilim* for his morning prayers. I pestered him to translate the prayers for me until he finally gave in. Other than the words to the *Shema*, the only thing I remember is a prayer in which Kalmek thanked God for not making him a woman. This text shocked me and soured me on religious practice, since I wanted no part of a God who was not even smart enough to notice that women are the pillars of the world, just like Atlas, the giant of Greek mythology.

Yet for as long back as I can remember, I always had an abiding pride in my Jewishness and a keen sense of my heritage. I don't know how my parents instilled these feelings in me since God was rarely mentioned in our house and religious observance was practically non-existent. We did not keep kosher or celebrate the Sabbath. Mama went to the synagogue only for Yom Kippur Iskor service for the dead. As for me, I was fifteen when I set foot in a synagogue for the first time, and it was not with my parents but with one of my high school teachers in Paris, Madame Liévin, who wanted to introduce me to Judaism. As a girl in my household, I was not considered important enough to merit religious instruction, and I received absolutely none.

At the same time our house was Jewish to its core, including even silly *shtetl* superstitions that both of my parents had absorbed in their own childhood. Without even mentioning so much as the Ten Commandments, my parents had managed to teach me the essence of Judaism, and I have always known in my gut that Judaism can provide me with all of the answers to life's mysteries, so long as I take the trouble to seek them out.

My parents lived their Judaism quietly through their deeds. A few years ago, as I read a quote from Micah, in the Book of Prophets, for the first time, I had a flash of instant recognition. Like the words to a familiar melody, I heard the echo of my parents' Judaism: 'What does the Lord require of thee but to do justice and to love kindness and to walk humbly with thy God?'

12   On to France

In March of 1948 we left the city of my birth, where my ancestors had dwelt for 500 years. We took with us a small pouch of earth from Grandmother Schreiber's grave.

We traveled in a train that brought us to France via Czechoslovakia and Germany. I saw my very first Americans when we stopped at the Nuremberg station in the American occupation zone in Germany. A detachment of military police posted along the platform, they were huge, beefy creatures wearing MP armbands and shiny white helmets that looked like inverted mixing bowls. They stood relaxed, with their arms held behind their backs and their legs splayed. A few were chewing gum, a form of bored, continuous mastication that I associated with cows and had never before seen in humans, since gum-chewing was anathema in communist countries.

After about two days of travel, we stopped at the French border in Strasbourg. A customs officer flanked by two policemen entered our compartment while two other policemen were waiting in the corridor. I couldn't understand a single word of the conversation between my parents and the customs official. The exchange – which on my parents' side consisted mostly of hand waving – seemed pleasant enough. There was some light bantering before the official returned our papers to us with a smile and a salute. (What a contrast to the Polish border police who had harassed us and methodically ransacked our luggage!)

'What did the customs man say, what did he say?' I demanded to know.

'He said "I see that you have a transit visa, but don't worry. I can bet that you will stay here with us for good"' Mama told me with a twinkle in her eye.

It seems that the customs official had guessed what my

parents had in mind, namely a transmutation of our transit visa through France into a permanent residency permit. As things stood, we held an immigration visa to Chile plus a transit visa that entitled us to remain in France for up to three months. We were supposed to board a ship bound for South America at the French port of Le Havre.

It was fairly easy to buy immigration visas to South American countries. If I remember correctly, our Chilean visas cost us $50, slipped discreetly to an enterprising consular employee. Of course, we had not the slightest intention of burying ourselves in Chile, but an immigration visa to France was an altogether different matter and beggars can't be choosy.

Uncle Menek greeted us at the Gare de l'Est station in Paris. The Schreibers were themselves in transit through France on their way to Argentina, where Mama's two sisters were already settled in the capital city of Buenos Aires.

The Schiff brothers were in Paris as well. About a week or two after our arrival we celebrated Duduś' wedding to Lusia, a survivor from Kraków, and then the Schiffs all left for Palestine. They arrived just in time to enlist in the war for Israel's independence, after six Arab armies attacked the tiny beleaguered country from all sides.

The Landaus and their nephew Tulek were still in England, but they too would soon leave for Israel. Great-aunt Sarah and her two daughters were languishing in a DP camp in Germany, still waiting for immigration to the United States under the minuscule State Department quota for refugees.

Once again we were all scattered to the four winds, yet this time one might think that we were scattering out of our own free will. But were we? Though the topic was never discussed, I know that my parents did not follow Mama's siblings to Argentina because they could not stomach the prospect of living in a South American dictatorship. On the other hand, hoping to join Uncle Wilek in New York, they had applied for immigration to the United States while we were still living in Poland. In spite of Uncle Wilek's best efforts and the impressive affidavits provided by distant friends who were willing to sponsor us, it soon became apparent that our prospects for an American visa were almost nil. Applicants who had resided in the Soviet Union were automatically suspect in the eyes of the State Department. There was an eerie parallel between the two Cold War giants. The Soviets looked at one who had been to the West and saw a spy; the Americans looked at one who had lived in the Soviet Union and saw a communist.

This attitude was so pervasive in the United States that it endured even after Stalin's death and the demise of McCarthyism. I can attest to this on the basis of personal experience. In 1960, twelve years after my arrival in Paris, my brand-new husband and I, planning a two-year stay in America, applied for US visas at the American embassy in Paris. The paperwork included a lengthy questionnaire, more than 30 questions, of which three stand out in my recollection: 'Are you or have you ever been a communist? Are you feeble-minded? Are you a prostitute?'

These questions enraged me so much that I was about to reply in a fiery paragraph entitled, 'Yes, I am a feeble-minded communist prostitute', until reason prevailed and I dutifully ticked the 'No' box next to the offensive questions.

The questionnaire was followed by a visit to the embassy doctor. Like every doctor before him – and I had seen a different one every year during our compulsory medical check-ups at school – he was intrigued by a scar on my right shoulder blade. The result of a huge abscess due to malnutrition in Kambarka, it was still a bit raw and looked like a shrapnel wound. The French doctors invariably asked, 'And what is this scar?' And I would always answer, 'Oh, it's from the war.'

The French doctors were always satisfied, but not the US embassy doctor. 'Which war?' he asked.

Still smarting from the 'feeble-minded communist prostitute' questions, I almost answered, 'The Great Patriotic War' – a dead give-away for a communist. But I bit my tongue and replied, 'World War II', in my sweetest tone of voice. (Did the man imagine that I was fighting in World War I?)

'Oh, did the Germans shoot at you?' asked the doctor.

I should have said, 'Yes', because the Germans did shoot at me when we were fleeing to the east in September of 1939, but I said, 'No, we were in Russia.'

A gleam of excitement appeared in the doctor's eyes. I could almost hear him thinking 'Aha! I may have caught myself a commie!', so I hastened to add: 'We were deported to a concentration camp in Russia because my father was opposed to communism.'

'You poor thing!' said the doctor, and my visa was approved in no time. Of course, the year 1960 was squarely in the post-Sputnik era when the United States was trying to catch up with the Soviets in space, and my husband was a scientist with an advanced degree – a coveted man indeed!

However, back in 1947, when my parents were applying for immigration to America we did not stand a chance. Thus we ended up instead with a transit visa through France. We were living in a small hotel, l'Hôtel Commodore, located on a street close to the Folies Bergère. To celebrate our escape from Poland, my straitlaced parents took me to that famous girlie-show and so I began my education in France by watching a parade of naked ladies decorated with feathers and tinsel.

Our tiny hotel room was furnished with a double bed, a minuscule table, one chair, one armoire, and a sink. Our suitcases were piled on top of the armoire. A folding cot that was taken out at night just barely squeezed between the bed and the armoire.

Though we were ostensibly forbidden to cook in the room, Mama cooked all our meals on a tiny alcohol burner. The hotel owner turned a blind eye so long as we did not make a mess. And she did us another big favor; she did not report us to the health inspector when I came down with the measles. She could have been fined for endangering public health, but she knew that we had no other place to stay. So she simply told Mama: 'You know, Madame Blattberg, I don't think that you need the maid coming to your room for the next week or so. If you need clean towels, *eh bien*! you can come down to get them yourself.' A typical Parisian, our hotelier embodied the attitude of 'live and let live' that makes the French at the same time so infuriating and so endearing.

I did not go to school for the first three weeks because we arrived in Paris just before the two-week Easter break. Instead,

I spent most of my days in our hotel room, teaching myself French with an almost maniacal determination. Mama bought at a second-hand bookstall a *Petit Larousse Illustré*, the French equivalent of the *Webster's Dictionary*, and an old copy of *Les Bons Enfants* [The Good Children], by la Comtesse de Ségur. The good countess was renowned for her saccharine books for girls. *Les Bons Enfants* was particularly cloying, but this did not bother me, as I found the illustrations that showed little girls in velvet frocks and lacy bloomers, and little boys rolling hoops, absolutely hilarious. The book was my Rosetta stone which I painstakingly deciphered, word by word. I would look up each word in my French–Polish dictionary and then crosscheck it in the *Petit Larousse*, where the illustrations turned out to be very helpful. The conjugation of French verbs was a total nightmare, but at the end of three weeks I had some comprehension of written French and a reasonable idea of its crazy spelling. Unfortunately, I could not speak it, since la Comtesse de Ségur was silent on the topic of pronunciation.

When school resumed after Easter break, I was placed in a class of first-graders, an utter humiliation for an eleven-year-old who was very tall for her age. However, my teacher turned out to be very helpful. Busy as she was with her 30 first-graders, she always found a few minutes for me. We communicated mostly in English, which I could speak a little better than French because my parents had hired for me an English tutor in Kraków, when they were still hoping to go to America.

I stayed in that class of seven-year-olds at least until the end of May, if not longer. Mother's Day in France always falls on the last Sunday in May, and I distinctly remember my teacher helping me to write a card for Mama. It was my first composition in French. Shortly before the end of the school year, I was moved to just below my grade level. I worked incredibly hard, perhaps harder than I have ever worked in my life, to learn French literature, history and geography, and to adjust to my new environment.

In the meantime, and after countless hours of standing in line at the Préfecture de police, my parents had indeed achieved the transmutation of our transit visa into a permanent residency permit, just as the customs officer at the Strasbourg border had predicted. We were granted the status of '*Refugiés apatrides*' – stateless refugees. Papa received a work permit and the three of us found shelter under the huge umbrella of French social welfare.

Food was still rationed. We received the same booklets of ration coupons as the native Frenchmen. My fondest recollection is of the coupon for *chocolat à croquer* – a dark, sweet chocolate that French children ate for their *goûter*, their afternoon snack. Two or three squares of *chocolat à croquer* munched with a piece of baguette made a wonderful *goûter*.

Children of my age were entitled to a quarter of a liter of milk per day. I remember going to the nearby dairy store every day with my little bottle and my coupon. The grocer first filled a quarter liter measure (a long-handled ladle with a flat bottom) by dipping it into a big dairy can. Next she poured out my milk into my little bottle. Huge mounds of butter and a dazzling variety of cheeses filled the store with their heavenly fragrance. Unfortunately, we were living on our meager savings from Kraków and we could not afford to buy such delicacies.

We were sent for medical check-ups. The doctor listened to my lungs and declared that I should spend the two months of summer vacation in the countryside, for the fresh air and the more plentiful food that would be offered in a farm setting. The city of Paris paid to send me to a farm in the Auvergne (the mountainous center of France) during July and August, and so it was that, together with a large group of children, I took the train to Aurillac.

We were farmed out in twos and threes to various outlying villages. A girl named Nicole and I ended up at the poorest farm in our village. Monsieur and Madame Castanier, our hosts, owned only two cows, and a tiny piece of land to match, while the other farmers owned a dozen cows or more. The Castaniers lived in a small two-room hut with two of their six daughters and Madame Castanier's father, whom everyone called Pépé [Gramps]. Four of the Castanier daughters, who were already married, lived nearby. Nicole and I slept in one of the two beds in the backroom and the two youngest Castanier girls in the other. The parents and Pépé slept in the front room, which was also the kitchen and the parlor.

Were it not for the swarms of bedbugs that devoured my flesh at night, I would have adjusted instantly to life at the Castanier farm. Incredibly, the bedbugs, who nested in hollows in the frame and headboard of our bed, did not bother Nicole. She slept blissfully through the night while I was being eaten alive by this foul-smelling vermin. I wrote a desperate cry for help to my parents and Mama sent me by return mail a round cardboard container filled to the brim with a white powder called DDT. I sprinkled this miraculous substance all over my bed and on my pillow. The bedbugs retreated, and for the remainder of my stay I slept like a log, wallowing in DDT.

The Castaniers considered Nicole and me with a bit of amazement because we brushed our teeth and tried to wash every morning. A few days after our arrival, we requested a bath. Madame Castanier heated a cauldron of water in the hearth and filled a wooden tub that was placed outdoors. I went in first and then Nicole followed me into the soapy water. The two Castanier girls washed next in the same water, which was getting blacker and blacker by the minute. It was so much fun that we made a weekly ritual of this communal bath, taking turns at going first into the clean water.

On the first Sunday after our arrival, the Castanier clan and Nicole went to mass at the village church. No one tried to entice me to go with them or made me feel uncomfortable in any way. Given my experience in Poland, I had been dreading that first Sunday morning and the Castaniers' reaction to a Jewish guest, but my fears turned out to be entirely groundless. Yet we were staying in one of the poorest and most backward areas of France, where many peasants were still convinced that Jews had cloven hoofs in lieu of feet. In contrast to the secular atmosphere that prevailed in Paris, Catholicism was still central to my villagers' life and 'Monsieur le Curé', the village priest, was the arbiter of everyone's existence. Despite this, I was never once made to feel uneasy.

Madame Castanier and Pépé were totally illiterate. Monsieur Castanier could read and write a little, roughly at fourth-grade level, while all the girls went to the village school under the French system that prevailed at the time – compulsory universal education until the age of fourteen.

Ignorant though they were, the Castaniers had an innate sensitivity. As they felt that my parents were anxious about my welfare, Monsieur Castanier was delegated to write a reassuring letter to them. He sat down at the kitchen table on a Sunday afternoon and, with much groaning and chewing on his pencil, composed a one-page missive. My parents were ecstatic.

My hosts were also scrupulously honest. Madame Castanier, who was holding onto my ration booklet, gave me every ounce of the chocolate, sugar and other staples that were my due. While other kids, who were staying with some of the wealthier farmers, were complaining of being cheated by their hosts, I was living with an exceptionally decent family. When we left at the end of the summer, the Castaniers even gave me a present for my parents, six of those lovely small goat cheeses that are called *crottins* – little turds – because they don't look like much. Looks, of course, are deceiving. My parents' taste, however, had not evolved beyond the cottage cheese and the very bland cheeses of eastern Europe, so that I ended up eating all of the delectable *crottins* myself.

Nicole and I ate exactly the same food as the Castanier family. Our main staple was the delicious local rye bread called *pain d'Auvergne*. The loaves were as round and huge as a wheel. Madame Castanier used to prop one edge of the wheel against her stomach while holding onto the other edge at arm's length with her left hand. She cut thin slices with her right hand by slowly sliding a giant kitchen knife through the loaf. At first I worried that she would injure herself, but this never happened. She worked with a skillful, smooth economy of motion that was a delight to watch. For our *goûter*, she slathered a slice of bread with clotted cream. Since the two cows gave but limited amounts of cream, we were given our portion of *chocolat à croquer* on the days when there was no cream.

Breakfast consisted of soup made from stale bread. Supper was the same soup, enriched with stewed prunes, bits of salt pork, and occasionally both at once. Lunch was usually a bit fancier and it included some meat. Pépé was in charge of doling out the meat, which hung on a ceiling beam just above the kitchen table. It was bacon or salt pork from the pig that had been slaughtered in the spring. Pépé cut chunks of the meat with a folding knife that he always carried in the pocket of his work pants. When he had finished cutting, he would wipe his knife on the back of his pants and carefully fold it back again before replacing it in his pocket. He used the same knife to clean under his grubby fingernails and even under his yellowed toenails. He would sit down on the kitchen bench, remove his wooden clogs and clean his nails to his heart's content before wiping the knife on his pants and replacing it back in his pocket.

After a few weeks on the farm, I became pretty grimy myself, but I was thriving and came back to Paris in excellent health. We moved to a cold-water two-room flat on Rue de Flandre, close to what was then the huge slaughterhouse of La Villette. It was a poor neighborhood of blue-collar workers, artisans and small shopkeepers, as well as some immigrant families such as ourselves.

I transferred to a neighborhood school where most of the girls came from poor families. I refer to the 'girls' because the French educational system in those days was segregated by sex, so that I went to all-girl schools until the age of eighteen. Though separate, the system was basically equal. Thanks to the centralized and egalitarian French approach to life, every public school was funded on a per capita basis by the Ministry of Education. The teachers all underwent the same training and the same certification and the curricula were everywhere the same. Thus I was not at too great a disadvantage for living in a poor neighborhood.

The turning point in my education occured in 1949, when I took the entrance examination called 'Examen d'entrée en sixième'. The system is vastly different now, but in those days most children remained in primary school until the age of fourteen and graduated with a diploma called 'Certificat d'études'. The road bifurcated at sixth-grade level for the few who took, and passed, the Examen d'entrée en sixième, which opened the way to what was then an elite secondary school system of Lycées, from which one could gain access to higher education.

I took my examination at the Lycée Lamartine, the school that I would be attending in case of success. From the street, the Lycée looked like an ordinary apartment building. The school was hidden behind the courtyard, past a broad stone staircase. The exam consisted of a full day of written tests; actually, I think that it may have lasted two days, but I cannot remember. We were served lunch in the school cafeteria and then allowed a brief recess period before resuming in the afternoon.

Jumping up and down the broad stone staircase, I met a girl named Cécile Weil. She too was jumping up and down and, griping about the incredibly hard spelling test, we became instant friends. Cécile came from a well-to-do family of Alsatian Jews. On my many visits to her home, I was granted a glimpse of French bourgeois life. When Mr Weil returned from work in the late afternoon, he sat down by the fireplace in a deep, soft leather chair and read the paper while puffing contentedly on his pipe, as if he did not have a single care in this world. An amazingly ugly bulldog called Winston Churchill lay at his feet. My heart ached sometimes as I thought of my own father, who left for work at five in the morning and often returned as late as ten at night, and still couldn't manage to make ends meet. It was during that period that neighbors once brought Papa home after he had fainted in the street for lack of food. Most of the time, however, I was too busy having fun in Cécile's room to give a thought to the plight of my parents.

Goûter at the Weil residence was none of the plebeian *chocolat à croquer* with baguette. We ate *pains au chocolat*, rectangular croissants filled with half-melted chocolate, and one of the closest things to Heaven that can be found in this world. During Passover week we ate thickly buttered *matza* topped with thin slices of salami – a not exactly kosher but delicious sandwich.

During the two endless weeks of waiting for the results of the Examen d'entrée en sixième, I remained convinced that I had failed because I had misspelled two words in the text dictated to us during the all-important spelling test. I wrote *ravoder* instead of *ravauder* (to darn socks) and *scenette* instead of *saynette* (short skit). (I think that I will always know how to spell *saynette* and *ravauder*, even if I live to be 120 and forget everything else!)

I passed the exam and now had to commute by Metro to the Lycée Lamartine. Although I had worked very hard, my success was due in large measure to the egalitarian French system which had propelled a girl from a poor neighborhood through the same curriculum as afforded a girl of privilege.

Inasmuch as equality frequently borders on uniformity, I benefited from the French spirit of *égalité* in yet another way. We all wore over our clothes a uniform called *blouse bise*, a beige-colored smock with her owner's name embroidered above the left breast. A few exceptions were tolerated in the lower grades – I was among them with my ridiculous navy-blue *blouse* – but none in subsequent years; the older the students, the stricter the discipline. We were forbidden to wear slacks, silk or nylon stockings, lipstick, make-up or fancy jewelry. We all looked the same. Although there was occasional griping about this draconian policy, for me personally it was a godsend, as I was able to hide my shabby clothes under the uniform.

I was growing like a weed at a time when we had no money. All my clothes were home-made from cheap remnants of fabric. Were it not for the *blouse bise*, I would have felt an outcast in a class where most girls came from solidly bourgeois families and had nice store-bought twin-sets and fashionably pleated skirts. Luckily, Papa's business fortunes improved by the time I reached the upper grades of high school, just when fashionable clothing began to matter most.

The cookie-cutter uniformity of French postwar life extended beyond the matter of uniforms and school curricula. In a country where BCBG (*bon chic, bon genre*) [the good style, of the good kind] is of paramount importance, being different was *in poor taste*. To be a Jew and a foreigner was nothing reprehensible, but it was just somehow, well, *in poor taste* – something that one did not really talk about in polite society.

It did not take me very long to figure out that nobody was interested in what had happened to me during the war or in my background. Not that the French themselves said much about their wartime experiences. What had happened just a few years previously under the Vichy government was just, well, something that one did not talk about in polite society. Much better to buy into the legend that Charles de Gaulle had so masterfully created: the image of a France that had massively resisted her invader.

Add to the silence of society at large the silence that reigned in our house, and you can understand that neither the little girl from Kambarka nor the frightened girl from Kraków were ever granted a voice. The adolescent girl who now lived in Paris and spoke a flawless, impeccably accented French had defiantly lopped off her thick Slavic braids in order to look 'like everybody else'. Yet in her heart she remained an other, a stranger peering through the windows of her hosts' securely rooted homes while she herself stood at the mercy of the next evil wind.

She was almost blown all the way to distant Buenos Aires when the Korean War broke out in June of 1950 and the populace panicked, fearing a third world war and a Soviet takeover of France. While throngs of Parisian housewives were frantically stripping grocery store shelves bare of foodstuffs and household items, the Blattbergs were standing in line at the visa section of the Argentinian embassy. Firmly resolved to run away from home rather than moving once again to a foreign land and a foreign language, the girl with the lopped off braids told her parents, 'If you want to go to Argentina, you'll have to leave without me.' Fortunately, she was not called upon to test her resolve, as generalized panic subsided and routine resumed within a matter of days.

I came of age in Paris and then moved to the United States where I established a family and built a career. The memories of my childhood lay dormant for some 50 years as I kept busy juggling the multiple tasks of family and home, of work and the world beyond. In time my mother died, then my father, and suddenly I became the elder perched on the topmost rung of our generational ladder while grandchildren began appearing on the rungs below.

I opened the small paper box where my grandmothers' postcards had been hidden for so many years. I did not know it was Pandora's box until one day, without warning, that long-forgotten little girl with the thick Slavic braids came knocking on my door.

'It's me,' she said. 'I have come back.' And she began to wail. I just stood there by my front door, which I kept barely ajar. Inside, the table was set for me with candlelight and crystal gleaming. A lovely bottle of Cos d'Estournelles, my favorite Bordeaux wine, stood open. My house was orderly and warm.

At last I opened the door wide and said, 'Come in, my dear. Come in, your table is waiting. The wine has just been set out to breathe. Come in and let us feast!'

What else could I have done?

Notes and References

PREFACE

References
Concerning the Soviet conquest of eastern Poland and deportations to the USSR see (among others):

1. Jan T. Gross, *Revolution from Abroad. The Soviet Conquest of Poland's Western Ukraine and Western Bielorussia* (Princeton, NJ: Princeton University Press, 1988).
2. Yosef Litvak, *Polish-Jewish Refugees in the USSR* (The Hebrew University of Jerusalem Institute of Contemporary Jewry, Hakibbutz Hameuchad, 1988).
3. Keith Sword, *Deportation and Exile. Poles in the Soviet Union, 1939–48* (New York: St Martin's Press, 1994).
4. Albin Głowacki, *Sowieci Wobec Polaków na Ziemiach Wshodnich II Rzeczy Pospolitej 1939–1941* [Soviet Behaviour Towards the Poles in the Eastern Lands of the Second Republic, 1939–1941] (Lódz: Lódz University Press, 2nd edition, 1998).

CHAPTER 1

Notes
1. Endecja: National Democratic Party (Right-wing party notable for its antisemitic positions).
2. Jozef Pilsudski (1867–1935): Hero of Polish independence. Chief of State, 1918–22. Led the Polish army during the Russo-Polish War of 1919–20. Returned to power through a *coup d'état* in 1926. During his lifetime, Jozef Pilsudski exercized a moderating influence on Polish antisemitism.

References
For the situation of Jews in interwar Poland see (among others):

1. Celia S. Heller, *On the Edge of Destruction. Jews of Poland Between the Two World Wars* (Detroit, Mich: Wayne State University Press, 1994).
2. Antony Polonsky, Ezra Mendelsohn and Jerzy Tomaszewski (eds), 'Jews in Independent Poland 1918–1939', *Polin*, Vol. 8 (London: The Littman Library of Jewish Civilization, 1994).

CHAPTER 2

Notes

1. Mark Verstandig, *I Rest my Case!* (Melbourne: Melbourne University Press, 1997). This memoir provides a lucid description of *shtetl* life in prewar Poland and a well-documented account of the destruction of Mielec Jewry.

CHAPTER 3

Notes

1. The Generalgouvernement of Poland, including Warsaw and Kraków, comprised approximately one-half of the territory that was seized by the Germans in September 1939. The other half – Danzig (Gdansk) and the area located between east Prussia and Silesia – was annexed outright into the Reich under the name of Warthegau. The area of the Generalgouvernement of Poland was placed under German civil administration to form the eastern march of the Reich, its *Nebenland* (neighboring land). On November 8, Hans Frank was appointed Governor-General and established his headquarters in Kraków (Krakau in German). The region was divided into four districts: Kraków, Lublin, Radom, and Warsaw. (Mielec was within the jurisdiction of the Kraków district.) A fifth district, Distrikt Lemberg (Lwów), was added following the June 1941 invasion of the Soviet Union.

   The Generalgouvernement was to serve as a dumping ground for the Poles and Jews expelled from the annexed territories, but above all as a proving ground for Heydrich's SD Einsatzgruppen, the SS units whose main function was the extermination of the Jews. Six Einsatzgruppen were attached to the Wehrmacht within the General-gouvernement. They experimented with massacres, slave

labor and expulsions before settling on ghettoization and mass extermination. See, Lucy S. Dawidowicz's *The War Against the Jews* (New York: Holt, Rinehart & Winston, 1975).
2. Jan T. Gross, *Upiorna Dekada* [The Horrible Decade] (Kraków: Universitas, 1998).

CHAPTER 4

Notes
1. NKVD (*Narodny Komisariat Vnutrienych Diel*): The People's Comissariat for Internal Affairs (predecessor of KGB). Army in charge of 'internal security'. Known in the underground humor by a 'nickname' which is a wordplay on its acronym: '*Nieznayesz Kogda Vierniozhsia Domoi* – You never know when you will return home.'
2. The 'special settlers' were deportees considered to be 'anti-Soviet elements' but who were allowed to remain in family groups.

CHAPTER 7

Notes
1. Komsomol: All-Union Leninist Communist League of Youth (organization for Soviet youth aged fourteen to twenty-eight).
2. NSZ: Narodowe Siły Zbrojne (National Armed Forces). A fascist-leaning resistance group whose members frequently murdered both Jewish partisans and Jews hiding from the Germans. After the war, they were banned by the communist authorities because of their opposition to the new regime, but they continued their anti-Jewish violence, especially the 'train-actions'.

References
For information on Polish anti-Jewish violence after the war, see for example:
1. Sarah Blattberg-Cooper, *Remembering Mielec* (Mielec: Mielec Yiskor Book Committee, 1979).
2. Jan T. Gross, Upiorna Dekada [The Horrible Decade] (Kraków: Universitas, 1998).

3. Marc Hillel, *Le Massacre des Survivants en Pologne 1945–1947* [Massacre of Survivors in Poland 1945–1947] (Paris: Plon, 1985).

4. Joanna Michlic-Coren, 'Anti-Jewish Violence in Poland' (in *Polin*, Vol. 13, Antony Polonsky (ed.) 2001).

Appendix 1
Laura and Gusta's Postcards

The cards from Mielec, as well as a smaller number of cards from Grandmother's sister Gusta Gretzer in Kraków, were mailed between September 1940 and May 1941, while Germany and the Soviet Union were still nominal allies. Most are in Polish. A few are in German. No other language was allowed for correspondence and one was well advised to satisfy both the censors of the Generalgouvernement and those of the NKVD: at times the text is like a cipher that must be interpreted by reading both between and behind the lines.

In the cards that are written in German, the flourishes and curlicues of the old Gothic script are difficult to read, especially in spots where the ink has bled with the passage of time, and blank words or phrases appear here or there in my translation. Blank spaces also appear on occasion even in the translation of cards that were written in Polish because Grandmother and her sister Gusta were trying to squeeze as much text as possible within the space afforded by a card, often at the expense of legibility.

The sender's address on Grandmother's postcards is in German: *'Laura Blattberg, Mielec bei Dembica, Ringplatz 17, Distrikt Krakau'* [Laura Blattberg, Mielec near Dembica, Market Square 17, District of Kraków]. Each card carries four stamps: the post office stamp in Mielec, the Generalgouvernement stamp, a stamp from 'central processing' in Moscow, and finally a stamp from the Kozukovo postal district (civilian district nearest to Kuma). Grandmother writes our address in her best imitation of cyrillic script. Confusing the Russian word *'poczta'* (postal district) with the Polish *'norma'* (standard), she writes: Barracks 50, Lesoutchiastok Kuma, *norma* Kozukovo, Mariyskaya ASSR.

Mielec, September 24, 1940
[From Grandmother Laura to Grandmother Erna]

Dear, well-liked Madam: I have received your card and I thank you very much for remembering us and writing us a card about our poor children. Before they left us, we asked them and begged them to stay with us, but to no avail. We have received a letter from our Helusia (the pianist) from Lwów with an enclosed letter from Leon and Andzia written already from their present place of stay, but she did not enclose their address. I was convinced that you had traveled with them[1] and I am glad that you have managed to remain. I have immediately written a letter to a relative in Lwów, asking him to mail the children a food package and giving him Helusia's address that he may obtain their address from her and telling him that I will give the money here to his wife who is in Tarnów, but I don't know if he has done this. I ask you also, dear Mama,[2] to send me the children's address because Helusia did not write me back yet. I am very glad that at least I can have some contact with you and find out about the children because thus far we have not received any news from them. Have Mr Menek and his wife also remained with Mama and how is your health? May God grant us all to be reunited with the children, this is our only wish. We miss them so very much and would like to help them, but alas . . . We are healthy. I have recently visited my sister Gusta, also your sister Mrs Wassertheil and the Schwarzes, and even was in your apartment on Agnieszka. They were all supposed to leave but have remained for the time being.[3] The air in our place is rather mild[4] and we are not feeling too badly. Wilek is in Wilno. He writes that he does not have steady work, but he manages. He hasn't written me yet about Leon. Be healthy and hold out till the Good Lord helps us. Once again, please write us the children's address right away.

Blattbergowa, who wishes you well

1. I.e. that you had been deported to the Soviet Union.
2. A prewar way of addressing an 'in-law' if one wanted to use an address less formal than 'Dear Madam'.
3. They have not yet been expelled.
4. Refers to the relative lull in persecution at that particular time.

Mielec October 7, 1940

My dearest children. We have received your letter that Neuhof has forwarded[1] and we are extremely glad that we can manage to be in contact with him and that he is sending you some foodstuffs that you need. I have already written to a number of people asking them to send you packages but I don't know if anyone has done anything. Our biggest anxiety is only about you. If it did have to happen this way then do take consolation in the thought that this will pass and we'll rejoice together again. Only try your best to remain healthy, to live through this. And you, Leon, with your sensitivity to everything. You are not writing what is your work, what is the climate there and in what direction this place is located. Do you have sufficiently warm clothes, and sweet little Ritusia, how is she faring there? Certainly quite a little miss already, write about her. Babunia asked and begged you to remain with us. Do not worry about us, we are healthy, only we think about you constantly and are trying to arrange that you may be where Andzia's mama is.[2] So far we have received nothing from Gliny[3] but hope to get some staples. Gusta is still in Kraków for the time being, her things are here, who knows how things will be. We have enough to sustain our needs and are feeling fine. We have recently received four postcards that we wrote you (they were returned). The Hermeles[4] are with their uncle. Tato[5] will write separately because we are not allowed [to write] together. Write details about how you spend your time there and what are your conditions and about sweet Rituśka, and most of all about your health. I am simultaneously writing to Neuhof. Why doesn't Andzia add a few lines? Dear Andzia, write a bit more about all of you. You know very well that you are everything to us. Please greet Mrs Wassertheil.[6] May God grant that we all see each other soon. Be well and remember your health.

Your loving Mother

1. Jozef Neuhof. A young man who had been working for Uncle Szymek and Papa before the war, and who was then in Lwów.
2. Lwów.
3. The family estate at Gliny Wielkie.
4. Relatives from Mielec.
5. 'Papa': Grandfather Leib.
6. Mama's sister Janka, who was with us in Kuma.

Mielec, October 10, 1940

My dear most beloved children, I have been full of anxiety about your fate since June already because it was known that people from those parts make excursions into various directions.[1] During all this time, we were waiting for some news from you till at last Gusta[2] sent us a letter that Helusia[3] had mailed her, but again without enclosing your address. I immediately wrote Helusia asking her to send us your address, but have not yet received an answer from her. In the meantime, it was only today that we have received your address from Wilek and, of course, I am writing you immediately. Tato cannot add anything as adding something to a letter is forbidden, so Tato will write separately. I knew right away that you would be in some sort of forest labor because I had talked to a man who knows that country, hoping he might inform me more or less about your location. Dear children, I can imagine that situation, the main thing is what type of work you have, what the climate is like; do not despair till the Good Lord helps us. We are all trying to arrange for your return to Lwów. Mrs Schreiber and Wilek have also written that they are trying to arrange this. I wrote Fisch asking him to send you a food package; as I did not yet have your address I gave him Hela's address so he might inquire with her, and told him that I would settle his expenses here with Rachel.

Gusta is not writing you because she does not have the right identity papers which permit one to be writing. They were supposed to come to us, but have received an extension of their residency. I recently went to visit her. We are receiving news from Wilek fairly often. My dear children, do not worry about us, we have enough for our needs, and our only wish is to see you. Write a bit more about you, how is your health, what is poor Ritusia doing; it's good [that] she has Romuś.[4] How do you spend your time there, do you have appropriate clothing? Write where this place is located, what is your work, and how you are fed. If Fish has not sent you the package that I wrote him about then write to Emanuel Straus (Lwów Kopernika 36/37) because I talked here with his mother and told her I would pay her here. Write what you need, what sweet Ritusia is saying and whether she has warm clothes. Please write us because people are receiving letters from there. Be well and console yourselves thinking that this will end before you know it and we'll be together again. I greet you and kiss you from my heart, you and sweet Ritusia.

Your Mama who loves you

1. Are being deported all over the Soviet Union.
2. Gusta (Golda) Gretzer, Grandmother's sister who was still in Kraków.
3. Hela Landau, Grandmother's niece, who was then in Lwów.
4. My cousin Romek Wassertheil.

Mielec, October 21, 1940

My dearest children, Without regard to whether or not we receive your answer, we write often so you will receive news from us, because I know how eagerly you await it. We have not yet received anything directly from you from your present place of residence, only some news sent through Neuhof to us and a letter that our Hela sent to Gusta. Gusta wrote me that she has received news from you. I know that you are often writing to us as well but we don't always regularly receive your mail. We write everywhere we can think of to arrange for you, if this is at all possible, that you change your place of residence to one closer to us, but we must all be a little patient.

Dear children, write us above all how you are feeling healthwise. Write to friends in Lwów and ask them to send you food parcels so you may have proper nourishment for yourself and your dear child. Do you have warm clothes, and how are the climate conditions there? Leon, what kind of work do you do and isn't this labor too heavy? Wilek writes fairly often saying that his brother-in-law is trying to arrange for them passage to America, but there are difficulties. I would be glad if this were to happen. I cannot enclose Wilek's letters.[1] Gusta has not yet come to be with us but I think that she will come. I wrote to Neuhof, and I will take care of things here through his mother.[2] Do not worry about us dear children, we have enough to get by. We have received something from Gliny. Write about sweet little Ritusia. May God grant that we see each other as soon as possible. Tato will write separately. I bid you goodbye and greet you from my heart,

your Mother

1. It was forbidden to write anything that had enclosures (but they could receive letters with enclosures).
2. I.e. I will reimburse Jozef Neuhof's mother for the packages he sends you.

Mielec, October 29, 1940

My dearest children, We have received your letter sent by Mrs Schreiber, but I am surprised that to date we have not received anything sent to us directly, notwithstanding the fact that you, Leon, are saying that you are writing to us directly as well. We are overjoyed at receiving any news from you, but saddened by your situation. We are trying everywhere to change that. I have also written to . . . [illegible, ink bled] and relatives from there and asked them to try their best to send you food parcels. I have asked you, dear Leon, what is the climate there and what is your work assignment and above all whether you are all healthy. The most important thing is health so we may all last through this, and God may grant that things will improve and that we shall all be reunited in good health. Oh, how I begged you to remain with us. Only keep healthy. If at all possible protect yourself from catching cold and rest after work and in your mind try to be content with your present situation and live only with the hope that all this will change for the better. Do not worry, do not despair. You can be completely reassured about us, we are healthy and we have enough to satisfy our needs. Tato has written separately. Gusta has not yet arrived to be with us. She has some things here. We have news from Wilek fairly often. His brother-in-law is trying to arrange his departure to A.[1] Write to us often, my dears about how you feel.

Dear Andzia. Thank you so much for adding a few words. How I would love to see you all, and dear sweet Ritusia already a little homemaker. Do not worry, everything will change for the better and we shall be reunited. We are feeling fine. Our only anxiety is about you and how to help you. I have received a letter from your mother. I say goodbye and kiss you from my heart. Please greet P. Janka and her family. Give a kiss to our dear Ritusia from her Babuniu and Dziadziusio,

Mama

1. America.

Mielec, October 29, 1940
[Written in German from Grandmother Laura to Grand-mother Erna]

My dear Mrs Schreiber: I thank you very much for your letter and the enclosed letter from the children. I shall utilize all the means at my disposal here to arrange to bring our children back. Alas, destiny has dealt us such a bitter blow. Our greatest worry is only about the position that the children find themselves in. That which has befallen us we could still endure it if only we could shield the children from harm. How are you, dear Mrs Schreiber, how is your health and who is there together with you? I am simultaneously writing to the children but have not yet received any direct writing from Leon, only via Lemberg.¹ I can well imagine your situation there. From here, one cannot send anything.² I think that you, dear Mrs Schreiber... you can...³ I have also to this purpose written my relatives. I don't know if you know about this because I have received no other letter but yours. Please... write. I am also writing to Neuhof, asking him to send a package to the children and I shall here reimburse his mother. Thank God, we are healthy. I thank you very much for writing. I greet you most heartily. May God grant that we shall be all together again. Best greetings for the sister-in-law Herminka⁴ and family.

Your Laura Blattberg, who wishes you well

1. Lwów in German.
2. Grandmother Laura was forbidden to mail us packages from Mielec.
3. Illegible, but must be about Grandmother Erna's efforts at sending us packages.
4. Mama's sister Herminka Diamand, who was deported as well (though not to Kuma). Evidently, Grandmother Laura thought that my Aunt Herminka was still in Lwów.

Mielec, November 11, 1940
[Written in German from Laura to Erna]

Dear Mrs Schreiber: I have received your letter with the enclosure from the dear children. I am doing everything that is possible in order to bring the children back from there, but as yet I know nothing definite. We are constantly tormented by anxiety about the dear children and we can well imagine their difficult situation. The main thing is that they endure all this without losing their health, especially now that winter is approaching and I don't know if they have any warm things. From here, it's not possible to send anything. I have written Neuhof asking him to send them some provisions. I don't know if . . . [It is good] that they are together with Mrs Janka. So far, I have not received any letter directly from the children, only via Lemberg. My sister Gusta has received some news from them in Kraków. Leon writes in his last letter to you that he writes to us often. The poor sweet child Ritusia, how she must . . . there; what can one do. May God help us to live through this and be reunited with the children again. How is your health, dear Mrs Schreiber? You should think about yourself to the extent possible . . . till God helps us. Please write . . . to me often. Where are your son and his wife? From my Wilek we get news often. It's not so very good there either. We feel fine, we are in good health. I have also written to our Helusia, [the pianist] in Lemberg. She has not replied. I don't know where she is. Do not despair dear Mrs Schreiber, God will help us, we shall survive this. Please give greetings to the sister-in-law Herminka and her family. I greet you and kiss you heartily . . . healthy.

Your wellwishing L.B.

Mielec, November 16, 1940

My beloved dear children, Notwithstanding the fact that we have not received any writing from you directly from there, I write you very often. We have recently received a letter from you sent from Lwów by Mrs Schreiber. I simply cannot imagine how you manage there now, nor do I know in what area is this place located and what kind of a climate it has. Above all, how is your health, and do you have warm clothing, and how does poor little Ritusia feel? Does anyone from Lwów send you any parcels? I wrote Fisch but I don't yet know if he has sent you anything. Write how is your health, and try your best to avoid catching cold, because it's certainly very cold there. How do you look? Leon, how are your legs, do you have any bandages? Save your health as much as possible and God will grant that we will all see each other in good health. Do not worry about us, we are feeling fine, we are healthy. We have enough for our needs, we have received a few things from Gliny. Only anxiety about you tortures us constantly. We have not received news recently from Wilek. I am writing him at the same time as I write you. We have absolutely no news from Szymek, and I don't know Binka's whereabouts.

It's good that Mrs Sch. writes us and sends us your letters. We are going to do everything we can to change your place of stay. Gusta has not arrived yet but will certainly come soon because she has all her things here. She could have been here for several months already. Wilek is writing you. He is trying to leave for A. but it is not an easy thing.

Dear Andzia, thank you for writing me about Ritusia. She has had enough adventures already in her short life. Does she have warm clothes and a stroller? Does she suffer much from all these changes? Does she remember us? How does she look? Does she catch many colds? She is prone to them. I already told Leon that I cannot imagine how he manages with the cold. Write to us through Lwów because we have not yet received anything through a direct route. May God grant we see you all as soon as possible. Stay well. Do not worry. God will help us. I kiss you from my heart,

Mama

Mielec, December 30, 1940

My dearest children, I have written you repeatedly and remain without answer, although I know that you must be writing and I know your sense of duty about writing us. As you can see Gusta is with us for four weeks already because she has been given notice from her apartment.[1] We had news from the Schiffs[2] that their nephew wrote from Lwów that he had news from you. Neuhof and Mrs Schreiber also write some news about you from time to time but we have not yet received anything directly from you from your present stay. I am trying everything possible to arrange for your return to your previous place of stay but nothing concrete has emerged so far. Write us our beloved children how you are faring there during the winter, which I can well imagine myself; whether you have enough heating and warm clothing. I would send you plenty, but alas. And poor Ritusia, how does she feel there, is she healthy, how does she look? Our biggest anxiety is only about you, about your health that you last through this with your health till God helps us. Do not worry about us, we have enough for our needs, we have received a few things from Gliny, we are in good health, we are in our [own] place and lack for nothing. Tato will write separately. We have not had any news from Wilek lately, but that's his way, although he has been much improved lately. It's not possible to send him packages either. It is also very difficult for him to realize his project of leaving for A. because he does not have a steady job there.³ Write us through Lwów and they will forward, maybe it will arrive here faster. I am sending Ritusia best wishes for her little birthday. May God grant us all to be reunited speedily and for everything to change for the better. Only write us about yourselves, about your health, which is paramount for us. I greet you and kiss you and sweet Ritusia,

Your Mama

I have been living at Lorka's⁴ for the past three weeks,

Gusta⁵

1. Expelled from Kraków.
2. The elder Schiffs, who had remained in Tarnów.
3. In order to get an entry visa to the United States Uncle Wilek had to prove that he would have the means to support himself.
4. Diminutive of Laura.
5. This message is hidden *inside* Grandmother's, to fool the censors, as only one person at a time was allowed to write.

Mielec, January 1, 1941

My dearest children, I am constantly writing you and so far without receiving any answer, only that which is sent from Lwów. As you can imagine, anxiety about you is torturing us constantly because we don't want to delude ourselves and well imagine your situation. I have written about this matter wherever I possibly could but so far unsuccessfully. They wrote to us from Lwów that there may be some possibility.¹ I know that you are certainly writing to us because I am well aware of your sense of duty, but mail is probably not arriving from there.² People are receiving mail from other locations there.³ Write to us via Lwów, dear children, because we are awaiting news from you every day. The worst is this dreadful winter, because here it is rather severe, and certainly there. What is poor Ritusia doing? I cannot even imagine all your conditions, whether you have enough heat, food and clothing. The main thing is your health. Gusta is with us already for five weeks because, as I wrote, she was given notice from her apartment. Write to us about yourself and Rituśka. We wish her health, happiness and change for the better for her little birthday. May God grant us that we may all see each other as soon as possible.

Wilek wrote saying that Mania[4] is again in Kovno[5] regarding their departure to A. He writes that it may be possible to arrange. Does he write to you sometimes? It is not possible to mail you packages from there, otherwise he would have done so already. Do not worry about us, we are healthy, we have what we need, we have received a bit from Gliny, we have fuel and clothing. May God grant us to be together as soon as possible. Ritusia must already be a real little person, if only there were health and other conditions. Keep up your health and strength as much as you can in order to last through this, the main thing is health. I greet you and kiss you from my heart,

Mama

1. I.e. of bringing us back from Kuma.
2. Kuma.
3. Other places of deportation in the Soviet Union.
4. Uncle Wilek's wife.
5. Kaunas, then capital of Lithuania.

Mielec, January 17, 1941

My dearest children, In spite of the fact that I do not have direct [news] from you I write often because I do know that you wait for our letters. This week we got a postcard from Guscia Schiff[1] from Tarnów informing that they[2] got news from [their] sons and that you added [a few lines] to it. Gusta has received a card from Kraków which you wrote in November with some description of your living conditions and Leon's work. As I wrote to you, Gusta is with us already two months because she was given notice from her apartment. We get often news from Wilek, he travels often to Kovno in relation to his departure to his brother-in-law. He writes that this is very difficult, but maybe finally it would be possible to overcome it. Mania also travels in this matter to Kovno. Gilusia[3] goes to the Gimnazjum.[4] Wilek works intermittently. He writes that he has scant news from you, dear

Leon, in spite of you surely writing, because in the card to Gusta you wrote that you have received from us three cards and a letter, while we have not had anything from you from your new whereabouts, only still from Lwów. How is your health? Guscia[5] writes about sweet Ritusia, her brothers write that she is wonderful, but unfortunately it is not given to us to be with her. Let us hope that everything will pass and we will be happy together again. The most important is, remember, to be healthy to withstand all this and that you could get packages from Lwów. Wilek wrote that from his place he cannot send anything. Do not worry about us, we are healthy, we have enough to live on and do not need anything. How is Andzia? I greet you and kiss you with all my heart. Kiss sweet Ritusia. Greetings for Janka.

Your Mama

1. Sister of Zelek, Kalmek and Duduś, who were in Kuma with us.
2. The elder Schiffs.
3. My cousin Gila, daughter of Uncle Wilek.
4. High school.
5. Gusta Schiff.

Mielec, February 2, 1941

My dear children, We have received your card written to the Hauptmans for forwarding to us. I can imagine your situation. I have sent you a package with clothing, some things for you, Leon, for Andzia and Ritusia. If only it reaches you intact it will be useful. How is your winter, because with us it is rather severe? I don't know why we don't receive news from you directly. News did come in from Recht, who is with you.[1] The main thing is that you be careful of your health, of catching cold because you are not used to this climate. Leon's current work is altogether not appropriate for him. Dear children, let us live with the hope that we shall live through all this and shall again rejoice together. What is poor dear Ritusia doing, do you at least have warm lodgings? How is Andzia's health? We have frequent news of Wilek, he is continuously trying to leave. Motek has also left Kraków already. We are doing fine. Write to us via Lwów. I greet you and kiss you from my heart. Remember your health.

Your loving Mama

1. In Kuma.

Mielec, February 6, 1941

For the first time, we have today received directly from you two cards from Leon and Andzia, which has rejoiced us a great deal, and at the same time we are sad for being so far away from one another, and for your destiny. The main thing is that you are healthy, thank God, and that Leon's work is not too hard. You do not write about sweet Ritusia, how smart she is, and does she still remember us. It's good that the climate is not too severe. As I already told you, I have mailed you a package with clothing, a few things for you Leon, some things for Andzia, a black dress, stockings, a bit of underwear, a scarf, and for Ritusia some undershirts and a kerchief. Please write to me as soon as you receive this. In fact, I want to send you Leon that suit from Borowie. You have others here but I'll send this one first, hoping that it will arrive OK. As for Uncle Moses,[1] I am simultaneously writing to him and asking him in any way possible to advise me how I can arrange things here and thanking him for sending you packages. I have written to him about this some time ago. I have also written to Kanarek, but he did not write back. I have written to Mettler asking if it would be at all possible to help you in any way, and he answered that it is impossible to send food packages from there, and he also very politely wrote that the one who is writing that letter knows you and he will gladly try to help. I have written back to him that I rely on him in every way because they wrote me from the Red Cross in Switzerland that it is possible to send parcels from a neutral country and maybe Uncle Moses could do it and this is why I had the idea of writing to Mettler. Wilek writes that he is continuing trying to arrange his departure for A. but it's not working out.

Do not worry about us. Tato will write separately. We are in good health and have enough for the most indispensable. Write which things you still need, may they arrive safely. [Write] about Rituśka and in general how you are doing. I greet and kiss you from my heart and sweet Rituśka,

Mama

As you can see I have changed apartment. What will happen next I don't know. In the meantime, be well,

your Gusta[2]

1. An uncle who lived abroad, most likely in neutral Switzerland.
2. Gusta's few words are written *inside* Grandmother's message to appear as one. For some reason, addenda were forbidden.

Mielec, March 17, 1941

My dearest children, We have received your telegrams about the packages. It is a pity that you are spending all this money.[1] The second and third packages we have already sent wrapped in cloth as required by regulation; we'll mail another one tomorrow. Was what you received in good order? We have received news today from Mrs Schreib.; she writes that she receives news from you frequently, and we only had direct news once from Andzia and once from Leon. She writes to us about sweet Rituśka, that she already reads and writes and is quite a little homemaker; a pity that it is not given to us to be together with you, but let us hope that we'll again rejoice together. We know that you are not neglecting writing to us often and this is why I am not asking you to write; the postcards that we received from you took three weeks to arrive. Write about Rituśka, does she remember us? and in general how she behaves in these present conditions. As I wrote to you already, we have recently had news from Wilek from Moscow that he is going to ride by Express train to Japan. May God grant they arrive safely to their destination. He certainly wrote to you as well. We had news from Binka this week; she writes that her only contact with Szymek is by telegram, that Andzia has sent her some things for the winter. How is your health and, most importantly, how do you look and what is your work? Write what things you need most urgently. We are healthy, thank God. Tato will write separately. Gusta is with us here. Do not worry about us, only remember your health, only get through the winter somehow. Leon, I have sent you some shoes, should I send some more? I greet you and kiss you from my heart, give sweet Rituśka a kiss from her Babunia.

Greetings for Mrs W. and Romeczek,

    Mama

1. On telegrams.

Mielec, May 7, 1941

My most dear, beloved children, We have received Leon and Andzia's card and are very glad that you have received the packages. As I wrote you already I've sent you a 10 kg package, a suit for Leon, walking shoes and various needed items but the package has returned, we don't know why. Two weeks ago we sent a package again, but smaller and wrapped in cloth, of course. It contains pants, a vest, pyjamas for Leon, two pairs of long underwear, one men's shirt, three ladies shirts, one towel, two dresses, three little dresses for Ritusia, one pinafore, one small undershirt, four handkerchiefs, two pairs of socks, two of stockings, one tie, one pillowcase, one cap. We'll send a package again this week and I'll insert a letter. Did you receive undershirts for Ritusia in the last package? It's good that winter is behind us. Dear Andzia, you write about galoshes for Leon. I have inquired everywhere, there aren't any. I'll try again. I am sending Leon's shoes that came from Krasinskiego.[1] They were already in the package that was returned. We want to do everything that we possibly can for you. We think about you constantly. The main thing is how you feel as far as health is concerned. I can imagine how difficult it is there for Leon as far as shoes what with his sensitive feet that were always difficult to fit.

We'll keep sending. Why do you write so little about your health and about dear Ritusia, how does she feel, what progress is she making and in general how she is developing? We have recently received a letter from Wilek from Tokyo, he is very happy with his trip. May the Good Lord [grant] they arrive safely. Does he write you? We have already mailed several cards for him to New York. Do not worry about us, we have what we need. Gusta is with us. We write to you often. How is Mrs Janka? Is she in good health? Be healthy, safeguard your health,

your Mama who wishes you well

1. Our former apartment on Aleja Krasinskiego in Kraków.

Mielec, May 15, 1941
My dear beloved children. We have received today a letter from Leon via Lwów mailed still back in February. Leon, you mention your trench-coat with the lining, but unfortunately I have not received it from Krasinskiego, but I do have other things which I want to send you and I do send things often. Neither do I have a suit for Andzia. Do confirm if you have received the most recent packages and we'll continue sending you others. We have

received today a letter from Wilek from Japan. He is very satisfied with his trip. We have received a card today from Mrs Schreiber telling us that Leon no longer works in the forest but in an office, and I am very happy to learn this. I am trying everywhere to find galoshes and I'll mail them if I can get them; in the meantime I have sent in my last package shoes for Leon, and I'll send still others. Write what you need most urgently and also what Ritusia needs. Write a bit more about yourselves and how you are faring. Mrs Schreiber wrote that you are sending Binka[1] packages. We have received one postcard from Binka but have absolutely no news from Szymek. We are doing fine, so far we have what we need. We would already like to hear from Wilek that he has safely arrived at his destination. What is sweet Ritusia doing? Leon writes that Ritusia will write us something. I am writing to Tarnów about the galoshes. Write what you need. How are you doing, Leon, with your poor legs? I can imagine how difficult it is for you to find shoes, and now of all times. Write what occupation you are assigned and how you are doing as far as health. Do not worry about us. I greet and hug you from my heart,

   your loving Mama

1. Binka Landau, who was in Archangelsk.

Mielec, June 1, 1941
[Written in German]

   My dear children, We have received your card dated May 2. To date, we have sent you five packages . . . One has been returned. Of the last two, one has been sent in April and the other on May 8 so that you probably could not have yet received them. We shall be very happy when you receive them . . . you need it so. In the last package there were for you, Leon, the 'transition'[1] suit and your shoes and other things that you need very much. We have also had news from Wilek from Tokyo but so far nothing further. May God grant that they arrive safely to their destination.[2]

   I shall . . . for Ritusia, I shall send everything that you have requested for Ritusia. I am so happy that you have such an accomplished child there, but alas we cannot see her. As I wrote to you already, my letters to Stanislawa and Fisch have received as yet no answer. I shall also write to Rachel. I have written to Schiff concerning the galoshes for you, but have not received an answer either. From Binka we have had news a number of times, and she all alone there. The sole purpose of our lives is to help you in some way. Mrs Schreiber has written us that you, Leon, are working in some office. Why haven't you mentioned this? Gusta writes seldom, I write often. You should not worry about us, we have what we need. Our worry is only about you and your health. We miss you so very much, you and the dear child. I greet you and kiss you with all my strength,

    your Mother who wishes you well

1. 'Between-seasons' (meaning for spring or fall).
2. Destination in America.

Mielec, May 28, 1941
[This card is particularly poignant because Papa wrote on it: 'the last card we have received from my parents']

    My dearest children, We have received Leon's letter sent via Lwów. As far as mailing you parcels, well I am sure you know how gladly we arrange for them and mail them. We have not yet received from you confirmation for two packages, and one has been returned. Leon lists some things we should mail, like the trench-coat with a lining, Andzia's suit and ski clothes, but we don't have these items. On the other hand, we'll send everything that we can, it is our most important duty to help you in some way. I have ready for Ritusia the things that Leon lists in his letter, a very pretty, warm long-sleeve little sweater and other things and I'll also mail whatever I can for you. I have written to my uncle and to Fisch in Lwów, they do not answer. As I wrote you already we have recently had news from Wilek from Tokyo and he also sent us a small parcel. We would already like to hear from his destination about his safe arrival. Mrs Schreiber writes that Leon is now working there in an office, and not like thus far. Is this true? I am surprised that neither one of you has mentioned this. Write and tell us how is your health, how our poor little Ritusia is faring, how she is developing, and whether she suffers from the conditions of your stay there. As far as packages are concerned, we'll do everything we can because we feel inside ourselves compelled to do it. I am saddened to hear that Leon had to sell his suits. I have mailed you two whole suits and walking shoes and will send more. Be strong and healthy, remember your health. Do not worry about us, I greet you and kiss you,

    your Mama

Kraków, November 8, 1940

[This card was written by Great-aunt Gusta while still in Kraków]

My dears! As I wrote already, I have received your letter mailed to ??, as well as not long ago a postcard dated August 2. Mama was here once in July and then in August. Since then, we frequently correspond by mail. Your parents are in good health, but they complain that they do not have direct news from you. Needless to say, anxiety about you is their greatest source of pain. We are doing everything in our power in order to help you. We have absolutely no news of Binka and Szymek. I am especially worried about Binka because I fear for her health. Her separation from Szymek was already such a tragic blow and now I don't even know where she is because neither you nor Hela write to me about her, though I have asked. I am making inquiries with Mrs Sprecker in order to find out something about Binka. Mrs Sprecker even sent me letters from her daughter who mentions that she has managed to say goodbye to Binka upon her departure, and again that she still had no news from Binka, and this gives me no peace. As I wrote already, Krysia, Sara, Agnieszka, and Sebastjan have left because landlords[1] have accepted them. I still live at the same address but, because another landlady[2] wants to take over this apartment, I don't know how it will be. I have managed to get identity papers. Did you receive a card from . . . ? Hauptman with my postscript? Do you know anything about their son? Does Mrs Ausfeld with her three children live near you? Her husband is asking about it. How is the climate there? Do not despair, keep your morale up. We are playing our part from here. Where is this place located, in what 'gubernia'? The Motkows are healthy and are remaining in Kraków. Maybe ? will be there. Here it is cold since September already. Mrs Gred . . . was supposed to write to you. I gave her your address. As you know, he [her husband] is in Yugoslavia. W.[ilek] travels sometimes from Wilno to Kaunas.

Gilusia is going to school and I think this will be good for her. Mania does not remember... I kiss you from my heart. Be well, Gusta

1. Some farmers have agreed to hide them.
2. 'Landlady' stands for Generalgouvernement.

Kraków, November 11, 1940
[Written by Gusta before her expulsion from Kraków]

My dears! It's been a long time since I've had news from you. I trust you received my recent large postcards. Your parents are healthy but are constantly complaining they have no direct news from you. A few days ago I went to visit Dr Nowak.[1] We spoke a lot about you. I am changing my lodgings. I am moving to your parents. Marcus is probably staying, 'the last of the Mohicans'. Myself and your parents are doing everything we can to help you (as I wrote already). Your parents receive correspondence from Wilek once in a while. Winter has started early. Already in September it was cold and in October potatoes have frozen in some areas. Fortunately, the harvest for this item was so huge that people are buying it not only by the cubic meter but by the cart-load, and even by the wagon-load. It's also relatively inexpensive. I heard that Ritusia is helping with the housework. You'll have much satisfaction from this little gossip. We constantly talk about her with Mama.[2] It's been a while since I've had news from Hela.[3] I am about to write her now. I have indirect news from Szymek, he is looking for Binka. I accidentally happened to learn that she is in Archangelsk but I don't have her address. Do you happen to have any news of her? Other families receive detailed news from their loved ones. You too please write how things are with you, where is your place located, what is the climate, etc. We can still find everything here. Did you receive some packages with food? I am visiting from time to time with Gitka's mother to inquire about Binka, but her daughter doesn't know anything. Mrs Wassertheil is also asking if I have news from you. Mrs Gred...sends greetings. Do you know anything about the dentist Gross? His sister wrote to you, and I have too. As I wrote already,

Mrs Ausfeld is there[4] with her three children. Her husband has asked me to write. Mrs Hela (?) has left to be with her parents in August already. Did she write you? I gave her your address. Mama hasn't been in Kraków since August but she writes often and she is very active. Please write to me still at my old address. I am taking this postcard to the railway station. I am greeting you from my heart,

Gusta

Ola Wassertheil sends greetings.

1. Dr and Mrs Nowak were Polish friends who lived in our apartment building on Aleja Krasinskiego in Kraków.
2. Grandmother Laura.
3. Hela Landau, the pianist niece in Lwów.
4. In deportation in the Soviet Union.

Appendix 2
Erna's Postcards

Lwów, May 25, 1941

Dear beloved children, Today I have received a postcard from you, Andzia, that was written on May 13; also cards addressed to Hela on May 7, two to Menek on May 10 and 11; somehow it all comes at once, the post is not regular; a letter from Leon to Hela dated May 1 came yesterday; many thanks for writing. I think my dear Leosiu that everything should be settled in the most orderly fashion, especially since you have no shoes. Andzia, dear child, as far as your misunderstanding with Janka is concerned, I am surprised that you are paying any attention to it; I am sure she didn't have the medicine and this is why she didn't give it to you; after all, you are good sisters, with a good heart to one another, the more so as you are in such an exile, orphans without father or mother, you should stick together, not to mention what is going on now when people are dying everyday; I only ask you to think about me that is left all alone, grieving over Papa, but I envy him that he doesn't see what I have lived to see, the children and grandchildren without me your mother.

As for me, I go downstairs quite little, my legs are very heavy, the stairs are hard. If only your deliverance came to you I would feel fine already. I have sent you, Andzia, money a long time ago in a newspaper. I also gave some to Basia that she should send it to you; also two books by registered mail, I heard that you have quite a library. Give one to Janka, so you can exchange. I sent the medicine you asked in tablets [Sreptocet], let it only arrive. I gave Basia some Salicyl, also in tablets, for sending to you.

That our Ritusia is so wise and sweet I have known for a long time already. Only one's heart breaks that one cannot see . . . our dear little sunshine. It's hard . . . but one must endure. Don't worry if you don't get mail regularly. You know where we are. Be of good thoughts, with God's help everything will still be all right, stay together, be healthy, so that I may still see you in this life. I have sent Herminka 500r. on 4/28. I must send her [some money] again, she is very poor with two children. I am kissing, my sweet little bird Rituśka very strongly . . . hugs,

Erna

Lwów, May 19, 1941

Dear beloved children! I have already confirmed your letter and the cards, I have forwarded the letters to Guscia.[1] I have received a card today from Herminka, dated May 1; she doesn't write anything about transferring to your place. It's unfortunate it's so expensive there, 3 r[ubles] for an egg, 2 r. for a glass of milk. She buys [it] for Anita and Marcel is jealous, but she cannot afford such expenses. I am telling you, my dear children, you are faring very poorly, but I am worse off because to see all this and be unable to help my own children, I would have been better off with you or Herminka, I am not a good mother that I have allowed my husbandless child to be taken to Siberia. She writes that they were vaccinated against typhus and there was some reaction; they are supposed to be vaccinated against spotty typhus in a month; she writes that Lonek[2] does not realize in what condition they find themselves, 'he [claims] I have beautiful things and live in a . . . house,' but he is sick, he doesn't know what he is saying; I am saying that Herminka . . . but he hollers that it's time [impossible to understand].

Here there is an abundance of everything, one sits at the table to baked goods and cold cuts, and my heart is bleeding for my dear children, this is what life is bringing me for my old age. This bunch of bachelors, they allow cooking privileges at Stap.,[3] but it's not the same as at the Sterns;[4] what can one do? Do you have better bread already, Andziuś? We have enough flour and eggs, if I could run over to the Sterns I would bake you some zwieback and mail it to you, my heart would be less heavy. Do you have a kitchen with a cooking top, does one slide the cooking pots into a baker's oven? Did you ever get fish there? If you want me to send you a package, write, tell me what you need, do not be bashful.

Do not write me about what I wrote about . . . ? brother. Hela[5] looks good, her appetite is fine, she is a good woman . . . I have

sent two books, they are not so nice, I heard that one can exchange books at your place. Give one to Janka. Be healthy. Leosiu, thank you for your greetings . . . I kiss you,
   Erna

1. Guscia Schiff, Grandmother's niece (and sister to the 'boys' in Kuma). She was in Tarnów under the Germans.
2. Lonek Diamand, Herminka's husband in Buenos Aires. I assume that Lonek was making every effort to send Herminka money and packages from Buenos Aires, but Grandmother Erna mentions only a rather crazy sounding exchange of letters. There are several passages of Erna's densely packed writing that I was unable to read and the reference to Lonek's letters is one of them. It would seem that Uncle Lonek was convinced they lacked for nothing, and that makes no sense.
3. Grandmother's current landlord.
4. Her previous landlord.
5. Uncle Menek's wife, who was recovering from an illness.

Lwów, May 29, 1941
   My dear, beloved children!
   I have received your card today, Andzia; it was postmarked May 19, the post is working normally already. I assume that you have already received the money because I put it inside the newspaper. I also gave Basia money to send to you, maybe it will reach you. As for Uncle Schw . . . , I saw and read those cards, I asked Menek to take care of it right away, [told him] I would give for all this 200 r[oubles] or more. He said it's none of my business, the cards are addressed to him, I can't talk about it anymore because he gets mad; this is how things are, I'll see what comes next.
   You are a mother yourself, may you live to be 120, you know what a mother would do for her child, though I am a very unfortunate mother, my heart is in enough pain for my children, day and night I have no peace, I cannot eat or sleep, with God's help we'll have peace soon. And now Andzia, do not torture this sweet little bird so much with recitations of poems, she is too little, at least leave her alone in the summer; in Lwów already the little child had to recite verse by heart. I'll try to get the things [you] left at Basia's. As for me, I go downstairs rather seldom, the stairs tire me, it's hard; at home there is the housekeeping; there are some of Herminka's housewares here, there is . . . of Mrs

S . . . Let's endure till all these tsures [troubles] of mine are over. If only I could be with my sisters in Tarnów,[1] I wouldn't know all that befalls my children and nephews. The address of Olek Nussef. is the same as that of Rottenb., I already wrote it to the boys, please remind Zelek of it. Zygmunt Schiff sent Olek a package as soon as he found out his address . . . really the poor soul doesn't even have a cent, . . . he can't sell . . . [then a few lines that are impossible to read] . . . my dear beloved,
    your Mother

1. 'In Tarnów', i.e., in the Generalgouvernement.

Lwów, May 29, 1941

Dear beloved children! I wrote yesterday, yet I feel like writing again today, maybe it's a conversation with you, Andeczka, from so far away. Gusta[1] was here yesterday with Heneczek, such an independent little boy, big already, he looks well, my heart is breaking when I see children in the street, I am literally dying from worry about where my dear children are. This Mr Janek Rozenzweig is not . . . , I am sure you poor things are penniless. Anduś, maybe you can air the sugar you received from Hela,[2] maybe this will draw out some of the naphthalene . . . , the fabric was in naphthalene. Hela earns very well, she has constantly concert performances, one also hears her on the radio, a capable woman. Write if I should send your shoes as well. Do you already have mosquitoes?

One lives in constant nervous tension, always thinking about an excursion to your parts. Several have left already, like Binka's brothers, they had businesses similar to Nacht's. Can one still get potatoes at your place? In general what are you cooking, is there enough milk, write if one can buy an egg. Where the mother of Hela Bir. and her in-laws are, a liter of milk cost 1.20 r. all winter, 1 kg of butter 24r., one can even buy a small bathrobe for 24r. This is a new Siberia; some medine.[3] How are our boys,[4] and Mr Janek, how are they managing? Zelek Sachs is working very hard. The mother-in-law of Guscia Maj told me that her nephew Silbiger lives with them. He contributes to their support, he earns 400r., she still must add 100r. herself to survive. What's going to happen when the boy goes off to military service? This is how things are nowadays. Menek works at a chemist (?), he earns 320r., he also works overtime, he earns altogether maybe 450r. You must already have received...child. Can one sometime buy a chicken to make a little broth for my poor little Ritusia...? Be well. I hug and kiss you,

your grieving Mother

Congratulations on your 8th wedding anniversary, may you live together 100 years... I greet you from my heart and send a big kiss to Ritusia,

your Hela

1. Gusta Maj, a friend from Kraków.
2. Hela Landau, the pianist. Papa's cousin.
3. Country.
4. Grandmother's nephews Zelek, Kalmek, and David Schiff, who were with us in Kuma.

Lwów, May 25, 1941
[Written by Uncle Menek]

My dears, I have received your postcards. Unfortunately, I cannot for the time being send you these packages because, as I told you already, I have no money. You well know that what I had is long gone for packages for all of you and the Oppenheims,[1] again cash for Herminka, Hela's illnesses, and I myself have been somewhat unwell, and the rest went for food. One earns very little, it's difficult to subsist, and it's practically impossible to sell what things we have. Mamusia constantly sends Herminka 500/month (also Jules has sent Herminka a great deal already). It's impossible, and I cannot take from Mama anything for these parcels because after all she has nothing more left to sell. If I manage to sell something I'll immediately mail you the two packages you requested with the shoes. Could Majer Bek or Starer loan you a bit? If so I would immediately make the packages and mail them – 200 rubles should be enough. Here nothing new [Be] healthy. I kiss you and wait for your answer.

1. Aunt Hela, Uncle Menek's wife, was an Oppenheim.

The last two cards were mailed to us in Kambarka after the war.

Kraków, October 23, 1945
My dearest ones!
My dear golden Andeczka, you cannot imagine my joy upon seeing an actual, personal live writing from you, because you had not even added anything to the cards that we have received from my dear Leon; I did not know what to think. Nor have I yet seen anything in writing from either Janka or Herminka, and alas so many years already. We only have telephone calls from them; Zelek Schiff also called, the poor man is looking for Hanka and Gusta, may God grant they still emerge from some camp. I have here my children that I am with them, and sweet little Adaś, he is a beautiful child, he looks like me, he has Hela's eyes, a fat... little body; this treasure keeps me alive. There is also Gusta Maj with Henryś, and Janka the wife of Rempel with little Ludwiś, and Josef Novotny-Neuhof; Romek is not [alive]; and that is all. We have a telephone...; Hela has no one, nor does Max, nor Gusta, what can one do? Ludwiś R. is staying with us all the time, his mother is teaching like in the old days; Mundek is in the same place as Sala, in Samarkand. The Papiers are without their Olik; Papier was wounded in the leg by a shell (fragment) in Warsaw, and he limps.

Come back my dears, do not worry about a place to stay. Your apartment is still here, but the mother of your landlady and her daughter live in it; your furniture is also there. We have a huge apartment, the Pilzer's apartment, there is enough room for all of my children together, if need be.

Be well. May God grant me to live long enough to see you again. I kiss you and hug you,
your Mother Erna
My dearest! We cannot wait till the moment where we shall be together again, given the rate at which our correspondence travels, we don't even feel like writing. We greet you, Hela and Adaś

Kraków, November 11, 1945
My dearest ones! Dear Leon, I have already confirmed your letters to us and to Maj, as well as several cards from dear Andzia, the first few words from dear Ritusia, a wonderful little

card. You cannot even imagine our joy. We have found your address in May from Straszewski, we have arrived here in April [April 10, 1945], coming from Krosno, we were liberated in September 1944. From 1941 to 1942 we were in Wisnicz, it was a hard nut to crack but we are alive thank God, it is difficult for me to write about it; we are alone, only one of my nephews, Zygmunt Schwarz, has survived as well as one nephew of my late husband, Milek Schindelman, otherwise nothing. Our Helusia[1] has no one either. Not Basia or her children, not Alexander or Basia Maj and her children, in one word entire families completely destroyed. Poor Dunek Landau has arrived here all alone from Romania, he has only you and the Szymeks, this is how we are. The Becks are no more, nor the Dr's daughter with her little boy, nor the Stachers. They say that one of the Sterns survived, Dunek does not know which one. Your apartment is there, the mother of your landlady lives there with a daughter, just return healthy and soon. We have sent you the '*vyzovs*', people are returning completely destitute. Ritusia... return... Herminka... be healthy all. I kiss you,
  your Erna

Ritusia, my dear heart, we have such a beautiful Adaś, he already has two teeth, he was born on April 20, 1945. He weighs now 9 kg, is a beautiful...I do not see Juleczek Gredy...There are no children. We are feeling fine. Edek[2] makes a living but my heart is breaking that my children have nothing. Edek has sent some money but it is a question when they will receive it. Uncle Herman wrote to me that Uncle Salo[3] and his children have survived, also the Schwarz boys. Lonek[4] sent a telegram asking how he can help the family. Leon's shoes are OK.[5] Agnieszka is OK.[6]

1. Aunt Hela, Uncle Menek's wife and the mother of my cousin Adaś.
2. Uncle Menek, who used the name of Edward (Edek) during the war.
3. Grandmother Erna's brother and other Schwarz relatives who had emigrated to France in the 1920s. All survived, reflecting the 75 per cent survival rate of Jews in France.
4. Lonek Diamand in Buenos Aires, the husband of Aunt Herminka.
5. Papa's all-important shoes, the very same that Grandmother Blattberg could not send us in 1941 because she did 'not have access to them', have survived the war in good order.
6. Grandmother's prewar apartment on Agnieszka street.